Abuse
and
Neglect

Abuse
and
Neglect

The Educator's Guide to the
Identification and Prevention
of Child Maltreatment

by
Barbara Lowenthal, Ed.D.
Northeastern Illinois University, Chicago

·P·A·U·L·H·
BROOKES
PUBLISHING C?

Baltimore • London • Toronto • Sydney

Paul H. Brookes Publishing Co.
Post Office Box 10624
Baltimore, Maryland 21285-0624

www.brookespublishing.com

Typeset by Barton Matheson Willse and Worthington, Baltimore, Maryland.
Manufactured in the United States of America by
Versa Press, Inc., East Peoria, Illinois.

Library of Congress Cataloging-in-Publication Data

Lowenthal, Barbara, 1927–
    Abuse and neglect : the educator's guide to the identification and
prevention of child maltreatment / Barbara Lowenthal.
       p.   cm.
Includes bibliographical references and index.
ISBN 1-55766-518-4
    1. Teacher participation in educational counseling—United States.
2. Abused children—Education—United States.   3. Child abuse—
United States—Prevention.   I. Title.

LB1027.5.L69   2001
371.7'8—dc21

                              2001035666

British Library Cataloguing in Publication data are available from the
British Library.

CONTENTS

ABOUT THE AUTHOR

Barbara Lowenthal, Ed.D., is a professor in the Department of Special Education at Northeastern Illinois University in Chicago. Previously an early childhood special education teacher, Dr. Lowenthal's research and publications have focused on attention-deficit disorders, learning disabilities, and early childhood special education. She is a co-author of two books, *Attention Deficit Disorders: Assessment and Teaching* (Brooks/Cole Thomson Learning, 1995) and *Preschool Children with Special Needs: Children at Risk, Children with Disabilities* (Allyn & Bacon, 1998). Dr. Lowenthal also is a co-author of a chapter in *The World Book Health and Medical Annual* (World Book, 1999) on attention-deficit disorders, has been featured on LD (Learning Disabilities) OnLine (http://www.ldonline.org), and has been commended by the U.S. Environmental Protection Agency for presentations about child maltreatment and the educational and health implications of childhood asthma.

PREFACE

Unfortunately, there has been an increase in the prevalence of child maltreatment in American society since the 1980s. Every community member needs to be involved in efforts to combat the abuse and neglect of our children, our most precious resource. This involvement has special meaning for professionals who work with these children. Teachers, because of their daily interactions with their students at school, have a number of opportunities to assist children who have been maltreated. They are eminently suited for this role legally, morally, ethically, and educationally. Legally, they are among the professionals who are mandated to report reasonable suspicions of child maltreatment to the appropriate child protection and law enforcement agencies. Morally and ethically, educators are responsible for trying their utmost to protect children from further pain and suffering. Educationally, children have difficulty learning at school when they are being maltreated at home. Interventions by their teachers can help them increase their motivation for school performance and achievement.

The purpose of this book is to alert educators to their roles and responsibilities in the identification, prevention, and intervention for childhood abuse and neglect. Chapter 1 provides educators with a brief history and background of child maltreatment in the United States of America. It also stresses the need for teacher participation in efforts to combat it. Definitions of maltreatment are discussed, and the signs, symptoms, and types of childhood abuse and neglect are described. Chapter 2 examines the possible causes of maltreatment, risk factors, and resiliency in children. Chapter 3 provides guidelines for teacher reporting of abuse and neglect and discusses possible psychological consequences for them, the children, the perpetuators, and the family members. Chapter 4 describes how a child's total development can be affected by the maltreatment, including the capacity to learn. Chapter 5 reviews relevant theories about family strengths and concerns as well as procedures for teachers to implement to assist family members to gain access to needed supports and services. Chapter 6 suggests social-emotional interventions for at-risk students, and Chapter 7 describes educational interventions. Chapter 8 is concerned with teacher advocacy for public policies that provide more resources to combat child maltreatment.

All children have a fundamental right to safe, loving, nurturing homes and communities. Educators, through their collaboration and work with the children, families, other professionals, and community members, can give hope to and foster resiliency in their at-risk and maltreated students. Teachers are truly part of the front line of defense against child maltreatment.

ACKNOWLEDGMENTS

I wish to thank a number of individuals whose assistance was invaluable during the writing of this book.

My dear and caring husband and best friend, Fred Lowenthal, provided me with constant support and encouragement, which led me to author this book. In addition, my children's and grandchildren's love and devotion were great sources of inspiration.

I would also like to thank my colleagues and students at Northeastern Illinois University for sharing their knowledge, support, and enthusiasm. My graduate assistant, Amy Britt-Simpson, was invaluable for her expertise in typing the manuscript.

My thanks also goes to Lisa Benson, my editor at Brookes Publishing, who simplified the writing of the book through her expert guidance, organization, and efficiency.

Finally, I am grateful to all of the nurturing teachers of maltreated children who motivated me to initiate this project. Their assistance enabled me to write this book.

*To all at-risk or maltreated
children and to their teachers who strive
to make a positive difference in children's lives*

1

THE TEACHER'S ROLE IN IDENTIFICATION, PREVENTION, AND INTERVENTION

"Sticks and stones will break my bones, and unkind words and neglect can hurt as much." These words, adapted by the author from an anonymous children's saying, refer to the hurt and pain that children who are maltreated often feel. *Maltreatment* is a general term that includes all types of child abuse and neglect. A more detailed definition is provided by the Child Abuse, Prevention, and Treatment Act of 1974, PL 93-247. This legislation defines maltreatment as "the physical or mental injury, sexual abuse, negligent treatment of a child or maltreatment of a child under the age of 18 by a person who is responsible for the child's welfare under circumstances which indicate that the child's health or welfare is harmed or threatened hereby" (p. 1826).

Because of their daily contact with the students in the classroom and their knowledge of child development, teachers are in a unique position to help children who are maltreated feel valued, respected, cared for, and safe at school. In addition, because of their familiarity with the families, teachers often can assist the family members in gaining access to the services they need to prevent any further abuse and neglect. This chapter provides readers with information about the history of child maltreatment in the United States, relevant legislation, the prevalence of this tragic epidemic of child abuse and neglect, the reasons why teachers should be concerned and involved in its detection and prevention, definitions of the types of abuse and neglect, and signs and behaviors characteristic of each type of maltreatment.

THE HISTORY OF MALTREATMENT IN THE UNITED STATES

Child maltreatment is not a new phenomenon. It has existed for centuries. Until the latter part of the 19th century, children had no rights and were considered the property of their fathers, to be sold, worked, loved, or abused, depending on their fathers' whims and wishes (Gelles & Lancaster, 1987). In the United States during colonial times, there was a deeply rooted tradition that parents had the right to raise children as they saw fit in the privacy of their homes (Vondra & Toth, 1987). In some families, child maltreatment was erroneously considered a part of parental discipline. During the 19th century, it was common to send abandoned infants to foundling hospitals operated by private charities. Older children, up to about age 10, who were poor and unwanted by their families often were sent to live in almshouses or poorhouses, which also housed adults with mental illness or mental retardation. In these institutions, such poor care was provided to the children that many died as a result of disease, malnutrition, unsanitary conditions, abuse, and neglect. It was common for those children who survived to be sent, when they were around 10 years of age, to families to be indentured servants or to be apprenticed as a source of inexpensive manual labor. The children were coerced by threats of beatings to work 12 or more hours a day. In 1853, the Children's Aid Society was created to rescue some of these children and send them to orphanages that had very minimum standards of care. Eventually, the child labor abuses led to widespread public concern and to the passage of the first Child Labor Law in 1916, which regulated child labor (Sattler, 1998).

In 1874, the first public reporting of abuse awakened the conscience of the nation. The report concerned a 9-year-old girl, Mary Ellen, who was extremely malnourished, kept in chains, and beaten daily by her adoptive parents (Gelles, 1993). Because there was no child abuse legislation at that time, Mary Ellen's rescuers had to use the assistance of the American Society for the Prevention of Cruelty to Animals in order to bring this case of maltreatment to the attention of the courts. Public outrage led to the formation of the New York Society for the Prevention of Cruelty to Children, the convening of the first White House Conference on Children in 1909, and the creation of the Children's Bureau in 1912 (Berger, 2000).

In 1935, the Aid to Families with Dependent Children program was initiated as part of the Social Security Act (PL 74-271). The program offered limited funds to poor, single mothers for the care of their children. Some funding, also very limited, was provided to the states to pay for the services of foster parents for children who were maltreated. However, no money was set aside for supportive services to enable children who were abused and neglected to stay with their families and to prevent further maltreatment. In 1946, Dr. John Caffey wrote the first medical report on his suspicions of parental abuse of six traumatized infants in his care (Berger, 2000).

During the 1960s and 1970s, there were more frequent reports by physicians concerning battered child syndrome and shaken baby syndrome. In 1962, Kempe, Silverman, Steele, Droegmuller, and Silver described battered child syndrome as a condition in young children who suffered intense physical abuse that frequently caused serious damage and even death. The word *battered* was derived from the description of their injuries, which included bites, bruises, welts, burns and scalds, pulled joints, bone fractures, and other damage to the child that resulted from beating, burning, or throwing the child or slamming the child against objects. The public reports by the physicians made the nation even more aware of child maltreatment, and, consequently, laws were passed by the states for the purpose of reporting abuses to law enforcement and child protection agencies. There still was a lack of a common definition of child maltreatment, however, and the states made few attempts to coordinate their reporting procedures. The time had come for the federal government to act.

NATIONAL LEGISLATION

In 1974, because of the widespread concern over child maltreatment, the U.S. Congress passed the Child Abuse Prevention and Treatment Act, PL 93-247. The legislation was amended several times and has emphasized that every segment of American society has a shared responsibility to respond to and prevent child maltreatment (Sattler, 1998). Table 1.1 summarizes this law and other selected child protection legislation.

The Child Abuse Prevention and Treatment Act created the National Center on Child Abuse and Neglect in 1974 (NCCAN, 1994). The NCCAN developed criteria for studies on the causes of child maltreatment and also disseminated information about maltreatment through their clearinghouse. Regional centers were established to conduct research concerning abuse and neglect, to discover more effective methods of detection and prevention, and to report on the prevalence of child maltreatment (Landes, Siegel, & Foster, 1993). At first, the American Association for Protecting Children (also called the American Humane Society) disseminated this information. In 1991, however, the National Child Abuse and Neglect Data System (NCANDS) was given this responsibility. Although each state had its own reporting process and specific definitions of child maltreat-

Table 1.1.   Selected national legislation about child maltreatment

Title IV-B of the Social Security Act of 1935, PL 74-271, provided grants to the states for protective and preventive services to children at risk and their families. Initially the money was used for foster care, but since 1980 some funds were used to keep children in their own homes.

Title IV-A of the Social Security Amendments of 1961, PL 87-64, provided federal funds for foster care parents to cover costs of the basic needs of foster children.

The Child Abuse Prevention and Treatment Act (CAPTA) of 1974, PL 93-247, gave limited funds for the identification, prevention, and protection of children who are maltreated. This legislation also created the National Center on Child Abuse and Neglect and a clearinghouse for the dissemination of information about child abuse and neglect.

The Social Services Block Grant, Title XX of the Social Security Act of 1975, PL 94-182, set aside some funds for the states to assist individuals with low incomes to access social services. Part of this money was used for child protection and the treatment of abuse.

The Adoption Assistance and Child Welfare Act of 1980, PL 96-272, provided funds to prevent children from being placed outside of their homes. The act also provided some money to help pay adoption expenses of children with disabilities who were difficult to place.

The Children with Disabilities Temporary Care Reauthorization Act of 1989, PL 101-127, provided funding for the establishment of crisis nurseries for children at risk for abuse.

The Family Preservation and Support Services Act of 1993, PL 103-66, set aside funds to help preserve families and to obtain needed services. This legislation was reauthorized in 1997 with the provision that states move children from foster homes to permanent placements as soon as possible. In addition, the termination of parent's rights could be accomplished in a shorter period of time, and adoption was encouraged so that children could have permanent homes.

Sources: Kemp, A. (1998); Lewitt, E.M. (1994); Lindsey, D. (1994); Sattler, J.M. (1998); Scheve, P.A. (1998); Ysseldyke, J.E., & Thurlow, M.L. (1994).

ment, each was responsible for providing some general information to the NCANDS about the prevalence and types of child maltreatment in the state; the genders, ages, and socioeconomic backgrounds of the children; the number of children removed from their homes because of safety concerns; the number of children involved in court actions; the number of those who died; and the relationships of the abusers to the children (U.S. Department of Health and Human Services, Children's Bureau, 1998). In addition, each state designated which professionals would serve as mandated reporters of child maltreatment. The mandate to report extended to anyone whose profession involved the care of children, including but not limited to teachers and other school personnel, truant officers, social workers, health care professionals, child care personnel, and employees of state law enforcement and child protection agencies (Lowenthal,

1996). Because teachers are potential reporters, they need a working knowledge of both federal and state legislation and contact information for local protection and law enforcement agencies. These agencies can usually be found in the local telephone directory under the heading of "Child Abuse."

THE PREVALENCE OF MALTREATMENT

Even with protective legislation, the rate of child maltreatment is increasing. The number of reported cases in the United States has risen by approximately 10% per year since 1976. In 1992, 993,000 children were maltreated (U.S. Department of Health and Human Services, 1994); in 1996, based on information from the NCANDS, 44 of every 1,000 children younger than 18 years of age were maltreated (U.S. Department of Health and Human Services, Children's Bureau, 1998). More than 2,000 children from birth to 7 years were victims of severe abuse, and as many as 1,000 children died as a result of maltreatment (U.S. Department of Health and Human Services, Children's Bureau, 1998). Children with disabilities are more likely to be maltreated than their typically developing peers. To add to this dismal account, these numbers may be underestimated by at least 60% because no one discovered that the real cause of many deaths was severe abuse. Although difficult to believe, parents and relatives compose at least 77% of the perpetuators (NCCAN, 1995). It has been estimated that at least 30% of the abusers were maltreated themselves as children (Hunt & Marshall, 1999; Vondra, 1990). The abusers can be from all socioeconomic levels and cultural backgrounds (Sattler, 1998).

According to the U.S. Advisory Board on Child Abuse and Neglect (1991), child maltreatment is now designated a "national emergency." This designation is based on three findings: 1) Every year thousands of children are starved, abandoned, beaten, burned, raped, berated, and belittled in the United States; 2) the system that the United States has created to prevent this maltreatment is not successful; and 3) the government spends millions of dollars every year on programs to deal with the results of society's failure to identify and prevent child maltreatment. In partial response to this failure, the U.S. Advisory Board on Child Abuse and Neglect (1991) has made the following recommendation with regard to teachers and other school personnel: The roles of all schools should be strengthened in detecting and preventing child abuse and neglect and in assisting the young victims. To stress the significance of the teachers' roles, the U.S. Advisory Board on Child Abuse and Neglect has recommended that educators, along with other concerned professionals, be appointed as board members because of their expertise in child development and often firsthand experiences in intervening against the maltreatment of their students.

THE TEACHER'S ROLE AND REASONS FOR INVOLVEMENT

Why should teachers, who are already so busy at school, be concerned about child maltreatment? In addition to the fact that they are mandated reporters, there are other compelling educational, ethical, and moral reasons for their involvement in the identification of, prevention of, and interventions for child abuse and neglect. Maltreatment presents barriers to learning in early childhood, school age, and adolescence. Research has indicated that the effects of maltreatment in early childhood can result in delays in age-appropriate problem solving, exploration, the ability to learn new tasks, and preacademic skills (Maldonado-Duran & Saucida-Garcia, 1996). At school age, the effects include difficulties in completion of schoolwork, a lack of motivation and persistence, inattention, disorganization, and low self-esteem as a learner (Vondra, Barnett, & Cicchetti, 1990). In adolescence, all of the previous problems could be intensified and may negatively affect the ability for abstract thought and mature problem-solving skills (Reyome, 1993).

Educational interventions that make positive differences in the lives of these children are those that build their self-esteem, model positive guidance techniques and nonviolence, do not permit corporal punishment, stress praise instead of criticism, emphasize cooperation over competition, teach social and self-management skills, and encourage the students in their self-selected interests (Abrahams, Casey, & Daro, 1992). Through this assistance, the children have opportunities to succeed academically and to feel good about themselves.

Ethically, teachers have expanded opportunities to detect maltreatment because of their daily experiences with students and observations of their growth and development. In some cases, they can assist families that are at-risk in obtaining the necessary resources, which can help prevent further maltreatment. Morally, teachers have definite responsibilities to report suspected maltreatment of their students. Thus, teachers have significant reasons to be involved in the identification of, prevention of, and interventions for child maltreatment (Berger, 2000).

TYPES OF MALTREATMENT

There are four major categories of maltreatment: physical abuse, sexual abuse, emotional abuse, and neglect. Although each form of maltreatment can occur by itself, they often are combined by the perpetrator. For example, before physically attacking a child, an abuser commonly yells, curses, or threatens the child, all of which are characteristics of emotional abuse. A second example is a combination of sexual and emotional abuse, such as when a perpetrator threatens a child not to tell their "little secret" or harm will come to the child and other innocent family members. The effects of maltreatment can vary depending on several factors, including the types of maltreatment and their severity as well as the ages of the children, their stages of development, and their genders (Sattler, 1998). According to a study by Sabota and Davis (1992), children who are neglected or sexually abused have elevated risks of death. Boys are more likely to suffer physical abuse than are girls. Children younger than 5 years of age are at the highest risk for injury or death resulting from physical maltreatment because their young bodies are not fully developed, which causes them to be more vulnerable. Unfortunately, children younger than 5 are more likely to be abused than older children because they take up more time and attention, which can provoke anger and abuse in some caregivers (Kemp, 1998). The following information defines each type of maltreatment in detail and is intended to help teachers identify maltreatment in children.

PHYSICAL ABUSE

Physical abuse is defined as inflicting injuries by hitting, kicking, pinching, choking, shaking, burning, and cutting or otherwise physically hurting an individual (Sattler, 1998).

Signs of Physical Abuse

Young children most often sustain injuries to their heads, which places them at great risk because of the fragility of their developing brains. An example of this kind of damage is shaken baby syndrome (SBS), which is caused when a caregiver shakes a young child so hard that blood vessels in the child's head tear and bleed. According to Case (1994), retinal hemorrhages and intracranial injuries can occur as a direct result of SBS. Indicators of SBS include cerebral edema, skull fractures, irritability, concussions, seizures, altered consciousness, respiratory problems, and coma. To be diagnosed as physical abuse, the injuries need to be consistent with SBS and not a result of accidental causes. Even if the injuries are not noticeable at first, they may cause later developmental problems in the child, such as vision or hearing impairments, mental retardation, difficulties in the acquisition of language and speech, and fine and gross motor impairments (Monteleone & Brodeur, 1994).

According to Barry and Weber (1994), a second common injury caused by physical abuse involves visceral injuries, or damage to the smooth muscles and organs. Injuries to the chest and stomach can be the result of the caregiver kicking or punching these areas. The death rate from visceral injuries to children inflicted by abusers is much higher than the children's death rate from automobile accidents (Barry & Weber, 1994). This can be attributed to the fact that perpetrators typically delay taking the injured children to the hospital because they frequently experience fear and shame and often are unwilling to disclose the maltreatment to health professionals.

A third common injury caused by abuse are burns from scalding and coming into contact with a source of fire or flame (Christian, 1999). Nonaccidental burns account for approximately 10%–20% of the injuries of children treated in hospitals (Simon & Baron, 1994). One characteristic that may help in differentiating between accidental and nonaccidental burns is that burns caused by systematic abuse often leave clear, regular patterns of the damage. For example, the caregiver purposely scalding the victim's hands and feet with hot water creates a regular pattern called stocking and mitten burns. In contrast, accidental burns usually leave irregular patterns (Simon & Baron, 1994).

A fourth type of common injury is abuse to the child's skin. Objects such as sticks, ropes, belts, and cords used to inflict injuries by chronic abusers often leave multiple bruises in different stages of healing that can be detected by teachers because of their different colors. Teachers can use the following color stages as a general guideline to determine when a bruise was inflicted: A bruise will be red or purple from the day the injury occurred until about day 5, green from day 5 until about day 7, yellow from day 7 until about day 10, and brown from day 10 until about day 14. Bites can leave patterns of tooth marks on the skin. Other types of physical maltreatment include suffocation, choking, poisoning, and drowning (Kemp, 1998).

Four criteria are given to assist Head Start personnel who suspect that a student is being maltreated (U. S. Department of Health, Education and Welfare, 1977):

1. **The location of the injury**—Suspicious bruises can be found on the following body parts: back, buttocks, back of legs, thighs, face, and the genital area.
2. **The repetition of the injury**—For example, a child has multiple bruises in various colors or stages of healing as previously discussed.

3. **The pattern left on the skin from the injury**—For example, a child has the stocking and mitten patterns caused by burns or patterns left by slaps.
4. **The explanation given by the caregiver or child is not consistent with the nature of the injury**—For example, the caregiver claims that the stocking and mitten burns are the result of accidents that could not possibly have happened.

If any of these criteria appear suspicious, the teacher needs to report the suspected abuse to the proper child protection agency (Berger, 2000). It is important to remember that when identifying abuse, teachers are advised not to remove any of the child's clothing. Only health care professionals should do this. Therefore, teachers will have the most opportunities to identify physical abuse if it occurs on uncovered body parts, such as the face, sections of the skin, and on the back of the legs when the child is wearing shorts.

Behavioral Signs of Physical Abuse

In addition to physical indicators of abuse, there are behavioral signs for teachers to recognize. These include frequent complaints by the children of severe punishments at home; extremes in behaviors, such as fluctuating between severe aggression and withdrawal; attempts to run away from home; early arrivals at school and refusals to go home after school; demonstration of extreme anxiety and fears; lack of discrimination of significant caregivers; poor self-image; refusal to change in physical education class; and self-mutilation and suicide attempts (Hunt & Marshall, 1999; Lowenthal, 1996; Nunnelley & Fields, 1999; Turnbull, Turnbull, Shank, & Leal, 1999).

SEXUAL ABUSE

Nunnelley and Fields (1999) defined *sexual maltreatment* as occurring when an adult uses a child for sexual gratification or permits another adult to use a child for sexual gratification. Sexual abuse includes a variety of behaviors involving contact and noncontact. Contact abuse occurs when the adult has sexual contact with the child. Examples are molestation with genital contact, fondling, intercourse, oral or anal sex, and object intrusion (Coster & Cicchetti, 1993). Noncontact abuse includes coercing a child to watch or pose for pornographic movies, videotapes, or pictures of sexual activities; making suggestive remarks; forcing the child to observe sexual intercourse or perform sexual activities; and sexual exhibitionism, in which the abuser exposes his or her genital areas to the child. There are other definitions of sexual abuse, but all of them agree that the child cannot give informed consent to sexual behaviors because sexual consent requires the child to understand the consequences. According to the Child Abuse Prevention and Treatment Act, children younger than the age of 18 are not able to give informed consent. The states, however, are allowed to alter this age parameter in their child protection legislation, but any sexual contact between the adult and child is described in both federal and state laws as sexual abuse (Landes et al., 1993).

The categories of sexual maltreatment are incest (sexual activities involving family members), pedophilia (sexual preferences for young children), exhibitionism (exposure of genital areas), molestation (touching or fondling the child's sexual parts), forced sexual intercourse (rape), sexual sadism (infliction of bodily harm for sexual purposes), child pornography (film and photographs that show children engaged in sexual activities), and child prostitution (children coerced to perform sexual acts for profit) (Christian, 1999). Abusive conditions can occur when the offender is in an authoritative position, such as a caregiver, and the activities are carried out by treachery or force. These conditions indicate that the perpetrators are using their power over the children to elicit sexual activities (Finkelhor & Dzuiba-Leatherman, 1994). The peak ages of vulnerability to sexual abuse are from 7 to 13 years of age (Finkelhor & Dzuiba-Leatherman, 1994).

Physical Signs of Sexual Abuse

There are a number of physical indicators of sexual abuse: difficulties and pain in walking, running, or sitting; recurrent urinary tract infections and problems with urination; bruises or bleeding in the genital, vaginal, or anal areas; torn, bloody underclothes; pregnancy in young children; venereal diseases; and regressive behaviors, such as bedwetting, soiling, and thumb sucking.

Behavioral Signs of Sexual Abuse

There are a number of possible behavioral signs in children who are sexually abused. The following is a list of some of these behaviors that can help teachers confirm a suspicion that a student has been sexually abused (Nunnelley & Fields, 1999):

1. The child has a compulsive interest in sexual activities and appears uninterested in other more age-appropriate activities.
2. The child is more knowledgeable about sexual behaviors compared with his or her typical peers of similar cultural and socioeconomic backgrounds.

3. Bribes are offered by the child to encourage unfamiliar children to be partners in sexual activities.
4. Other students complain about being coerced by the child to engage in sexual acts.
5. When the teacher questions the child about sexual behaviors, the child becomes fearful, belligerent, and angry.

Other psychological and emotional symptoms are common. Frequently, children who are sexually abused feel trapped or powerless to stop the abuse; have nightmares and other sleep disorders (e.g., difficulty in falling and staying asleep during the night); act confused, withdrawn, fearful, and depressed; are extremely aggressive and noncompliant for unknown reasons; act out with age-inappropriate temper tantrums; refuse to go home or try to run away; and behave in precocious, seductive ways. Additional indicators include a variety of psychosomatic complaints, such as headaches or stomachaches; lack of appetite; extreme mood changes; hysteria; mental illness, such as multiple personalities; and attempted suicide.

A number of these behavioral indicators coincide with the criteria for posttraumatic stress disorder (American Psychiatric Association, 1994): 1) child abuse is recognized as a significant source of stress; 2) the child reexperiences the trauma from abuse through dreams, nightmares, and thoughts; 3) the child withdraws from social relationships and shows a lack of interest in developmentally appropriate activities; and 4) the child shows signs of hypervigilance, in which he or she continuously searches the environment to avoid the repetition of the abusive event and any other situations that recall memories of the trauma (Christian, 1999).

DEFINITIONS OF PSYCHOLOGICAL ABUSE

The term *psychological abuse* is replacing *emotional abuse* because it is more comprehensive and better explains the affective, behavioral, and cognitive effects from this type of maltreatment (Christian, 1999). *Psychological abuse* is defined by situations in which the caregiver inflicts psychological or emotional damage on the child with the use of threats and verbal harassment that result in the systematic destruction of the child's self-esteem (Nunnelley & Fields, 1999). When adults constantly criticize, stigmatize, and belittle their children, this treatment can have harmful, lifetime effects on the children's total development. Children suffer as much or more from psychological abuse than from other types of maltreatment. Psychological abuse negatively affects their behaviors, feelings, and thoughts (American Humane Association, 1998).

The categories of psychological abuse include rejecting, exploiting, devaluing, terrorizing, denying essential stimulation, and isolating (Kemp, 1998; Sattler, 1998). When children are rejected, they feel unworthy and unacceptable. When children are exploited, they are coerced into inappropriate, self-destructive, or criminal behaviors for the purpose of profit for their abusers. Examples of these acts are gambling, prostitution, and the sale and use of illegal drugs. When children are devalued, they are criticized, humiliated, and made to feel inferior and not worthy. When children are terrorized, they are so terribly threatened that they become extremely fearful and anxious. If children are denied essential stimulation, their basic needs for nurturing, love, and attention are ignored. If children are isolated, they are unable to be with their peers and other more nurturing adults. In extreme cases, they may be locked up and chained. There are a number of physical and behavioral signs of psychological abuse.

Physical Signs of Psychological Abuse

Physical indicators of psychological abuse include eating disorders; self-abusive behaviors (e.g., head banging, pulling one's hair); sleep disorders (e.g., nightmares, night terrors); age-inappropriate bedwetting and soiling; speech disorders; ulcers; asthma; severe allergies; and developmental lags in the physical, emotional, and cognitive areas.

Behavioral Signs of Psychological Abuse

Behaviors that may indicate psychological abuse could be at opposite extremes. For example, children may be very aggressive and noncompliant or extremely passive and anxious to please. Other possible behaviors of children who are being psychologically abused include excessive seeking out of other adults for affection, viewing the abuse as being their fault, acting depressed and withdrawn, running away from home, having unexplained temper tantrums with excessive yelling and shouting, experiencing difficulty making friends and social isolation, being unable to appropriately communicate their needs to others, having low self-esteem, and attempting suicide (American Humane Association, 1998; Turnbull et al., 1999). Sometimes, children who are psychologically abused try to hide their feelings from others because they feel ashamed and inferior. Teachers need to look at children's puzzling behaviors as cries for help and try to find the true reasons for their distress.

DEFINITION OF NEGLECT

The last category of maltreatment is neglect, which is considered an act of omission by the abusive caregiver rather than an act of commission, such as in physical, sexual, and psychological abuse. *Neglect* has been defined by Polansky, Chalmers, Buttenweiser, and Williams (1987) as a condition in which the significant caregiver permits the child, either on purpose or through inattention, to experience unnecessary suffering or fails to provide for the essential needs of the child. All children need adequate food, shelter, clothing, health care, education, supervision, nurturing, guidance, and positive discipline. When these needs are not met, either because of the inability or unwillingness of the caregivers, children are considered neglected (Christian, 1999; DePanfilis, 1996). For some children, neglect is only temporary, but for others, it is a way of life. In these situations, professionals tend to focus on which needs are not met and how to help the family to fulfill them for their children.

Berger (2000) identified the following three categories of neglect: physical, educational, and emotional. Physical neglect occurs when the caregiver does not provide adequate clothing, food, shelter, and supervision for the child. Educational neglect occurs when the caregiver permits school truancy. Emotional neglect occurs when the significant caregiver ignores the child's need for affection, attention, comfort, and protection. Total neglect and rejection is abandonment of the child. Teachers need to be especially aware of the physical and behavioral characteristics of neglect as this form of maltreatment can have the most negative effects on children's school achievement and motivation to learn.

Physical Signs of Neglect

One or more of the following signs are possible indicators of physical neglect: The height and weight of the child is significantly below his or her peers; the child is inappropriately dressed for the weather, such as having no outer clothing in the winter; the child has scaly skin and dark circles under his or her eyes; the child is listless and has an apathetic appearance; there are obvious signs of lack of medical care; the child has inadequate shelter; and the child frequently participates in dangerous activities due to a lack of supervision.

A special category of physical neglect is the nonorganic failure to thrive (FTT) syndrome in infants and young children. Nonorganic FTT does not result from a physical disability but occurs because of the caregiver's failure to adequately provide nutrition for the child

(Munkel, 1994; Pecora, Whittaker, & Maluccio, 1992). Some general indicators of nonorganic FTT include weight or height below the third percentile; failure to maintain weight and to grow; delays in motor skills and in muscle tone; small head size; emaciated appearance; pale, mottled skin; and frequent illness, such as colds and upset stomachs. Behavioral signs of nonorganic FTT include eating inappropriate food, such as garbage; self-mutilation; hypervigilance, in which the child continuously scans the environment for danger or abuse; infrequent smiling; irritability; lack of responsiveness to other people; negative interactions with the caregiver; and resistance to being touched or cuddled (Munkel, 1994). Long-term effects from the malnutrition associated with nonorganic FTT may include developmental delays, personality difficulties, starvation, or, in extreme cases, death. A child with nonorganic FTT may require repeated hospitalizations to determine whether the child gains weight and thrives when cared for by alternate caregivers, such as hospital personnel. If the child is at risk for survival because of the lack of nurturance and nourishment in his or her home, the child may need foster care until the family is able to provide for these basic needs (Greis, 1999).

Behavioral Signs of Neglect in Older Children

Behavioral symptoms of neglect that teachers may notice in older students are truancy and tardiness or, at the other extreme, refusals to go home after school and attempts to run away. Because of hunger, children will sometimes steal, beg, and hoard food. They often complain that no one takes care of them and frequently become dependent on their teachers and other school personnel to meet their basic needs. Behaviors can vary from withdrawal and depression to aggression and conduct disorders. As mentioned previously, there is an overlap between behavioral indicators of neglect and other forms of abuse. The reasons for this are that often the types of maltreatment combine with one another and they have common characteristics.

Research indicates that many children who are abused and neglected, in contrast to their peers who are not maltreated, have negative reactions to peer distress (Barnett, 1997). Children who have not been maltreated act concerned and usually try to help another child who has been physically or emotionally maltreated. Children who are maltreated, however, react with fear, threats, and aggression to the distress of their peers. Other common feelings in these children include difficulties in expressing their emotions and in self-management as well as having intense feelings of inferiority, guilt, embarrassment, shame, and anger.

CONCLUSION

In addition to the information about general characteristics of child maltreatment, a checklist developed by Berger (2000) assists teachers in identifying abuse and neglect in children at different ages by having the teachers ask themselves questions. This checklist is summarized in Figure 1.1.

In this chapter, we have reviewed information about the history of child maltreatment in the United States, relevant legislation, and the types and prevalence of maltreatment. Chapter 2 investigates its causes and risk factors as well as the concept of resiliency in the children and their families.

At preschool age

❑ Does the child seem to fear his or her parents?

❑ Is the child often absent from preschool?

At school age

❑ Does the student demonstrate unusual behaviors, such as extreme conduct disorders of passivity and withdrawal?

❑ Is the student often truant or tardy?

❑ Does the student frequently arrive very early at school or refuse to go home after school?

❑ Does the student lack social skills and have difficulty making friends?

❑ Does the child appear uncared for or wear inadequate clothing for the weather?

❑ Does the child beg, borrow, steal, or hoard food?

❑ Does the child appear frightened of his or her parents?

At adolescence

❑ Does the student have frequent disciplinary problems?

❑ Does the student exhibit difficulties in communicating with his or her parents?

❑ Does the student try to run away from his or her home?

❑ Do the parents seem overly strict and expect perfect behavior from their child?

❑ Does the student lack friends and appear isolated?

Figure 1.1. Checklist for identifying abuse and neglect in children of different ages (From Parents as Partners in Education 5/e by Berger © 2000. REPRINTED BY PERMISSION OF PEARSON EDUCATION, INC. UPPER SADDLE RIVER, NJ 07458.)

2

CAUSES OF MALTREATMENT, RISK FACTORS, AND RESILIENCY

In this chapter, several theories of child maltreatment are explored: sociocultural, social learning and interaction, individualistic, cognitive, attachment, transactional, and family system theories. Just as there are a number of theories, there also are multiple causes or risk factors of child maltreatment. These multiple causes are described next in the chapter. Then, an explanation is provided about how child maltreatment can occur through the interaction of many risk factors that can overwhelm the protective factors (e.g., strong parent–child relationships, spousal cooperation) in the lives of the family members. The result may be child maltreatment. Next, abuser profiles associated with the different types of abuse and neglect are provided. The last section of the chapter explains the concept of resiliency in children and their families. Resiliency consists of protective factors within these family members that distinguish them from other families with the same risk factors. One of these protective factors is the role of a caring, empathetic teacher who provides children with a safe and nurturing school environment. This role gives teachers hope that they can help by being mentors to the children, which in turn helps to counter their maltreatment at home.

THEORIES OF MALTREATMENT

A number of theories seek to explain why maltreatment occurs. This chapter addresses the sociocultural, social learning and interaction, individualistic, cognitive, attachment, transactional, and family system theories.

The Sociocultural Theory

The *sociocultural theory* suggests that risk factors in the offenders' environments influence them to maltreat children. These factors include inadequate family structure, lack of necessary support systems, and social stressors (Sattler, 1998). Inadequate family structure includes dysfunctional parent–child relationships, harsh and inconsistent discipline practices, lack of control of the children's behaviors, and the absence of predictable family routines. Lack of necessary support systems can include not having access to the necessary social services; not having enough financial resources; having inadequate social and financial support from extended family, friends, neighbors, and community members; and social isolation. The families may have additional social stressors, such as unemployment, lack of education, frequent moves, and dangerous living conditions in crime-ridden neighborhoods. Cultural norms of acceptance of violence, lack of concern for others, and belief in the value of harsh punishment can place the families at additional risk (Tzeng, Jackson, & Karlson, 1991).

The Social Learning and Interaction Theory

A basic assumption of the *social learning and interaction theory* is that the family is a system that can produce adaptive or maladaptive behaviors through the modeling of nonviolent or violent behaviors. The roles of the offenders and the maltreated children are learned and transmitted from one generation to the next. When abusive parenting is condoned by the caregivers, the children accept it as appropriate practice when they are adults with their own offspring. This theory also suggests that the abusers tend to think of children as being objects rather than human beings. This belief leads to feelings of inferiority, low self-esteem, and helplessness in children (Schneider, 1993).

The Individualistic Theory

The *individualistic theory* suggests that abusive behaviors stem from differences in individuals. Abusive caregivers have different beliefs and behaviors from those who are nonabusive. The different beliefs and actions consist of unrealistic expectations of children, hostile reactions to typical behaviors of children, refusal to feel responsible for the maltreatment, placement of blame on others, belief in corporal punishment, and, often, substance abuse (Gondolf, 1995; Kemp, 1998). In this theory, there is an additional emphasis similar to that in the social learning and interaction theory that maltreatment arises from the background or history of the individual. For example, if the offenders were maltreated as children, they then will repeat the maltreatment with their own children. The abusers rationalize their abuse as necessary to improve their children's behaviors and to "toughen" them up.

The Cognitive Theory

The basic assumption of the *cognitive theory* is that the ways in which abusive caregivers respond to children depend on their thoughts about the children and themselves. Bugental (1992) and Sattler (1998) described the following thoughts abusive caregivers may have as risk factors for abuse and neglect:

1. The abusers think that their children deliberately behave to make them angry.
2. The abusers believe that the children are always in control of their behaviors and that misbehaviors are the result of their willful acts and not due to other causes.
3. The abusive caregivers believe that it is beyond their power to stop the maltreatment.
4. The abusers view the misbehaviors of their children as threats.
5. The offenders think that maltreatment is necessary to control their children's misbehaviors.
6. When the children make the offenders angry, the offenders may have unpleasant physical reactions, such as a faster heart rate, elevated blood pressure, and an increase in perspiration. The abusers blame the children for this discomfort, which leads to another cycle of increased maltreatment.

The Attachment Theory

The *attachment theory* focuses on the bond that forms between a parent or caregiver and a child during infancy. Researchers have described attachment as being the most significant early socioemotional event in a child's life (Lieberman, Weston, & Pawl, 1991; van IJzendoorn, Juffer, & Duyvesteyn, 1995). A secure attachment between the parent and child develops in infancy when the caregiver is responsive to the needs of the infant. Being responsive ensures the infant's survival as the baby is provided with the necessary care, nurturance, and protection. The infant is then able to bond with the caregiver who, in turn, becomes more and more responsive, which deepens the bond between them. Their attachment continues over time with each partner influencing the other partner's development of this process.

When children are securely attached, they view themselves as worthy of love, are self-confident of their abilities, and tend to positively interact with other individuals (Ferber, 1996). The opposite can occur when children are insecurely attached. Because they are not loved, they feel unworthy, inferior, and have problems relating to other people. They seem to expect rejection, which then fosters the actual rejection of their peers. Children who are maltreated are especially vulnerable to attachment disorders, which result in difficulties in showing affection, seeking help, cooperating, controlling their behaviors, and feeling safe to learn from school and other experiences. Because of these difficulties, attachment disorders can lead to social isolation, loss of motivation to achieve at school, withdrawal, and aggression. Children who are maltreated also have inadequate opportunities to learn appropriate social skills because of the negative modeling of their caregivers (Morrison, Frank, Holland, & Kates, 1999).

The Transactional Theory

The *transactional theory* emphasizes the relationships between the parent or caregiver and the child as well as between all of the family members and the wider social community. Child development is viewed as a complex and dynamic system of transactions in which children, parents, family members, and other individuals in the social environment both influence and are influenced by each other (Christian, 1999). There needs to be a good fit between the characteristics of the child and those of the caregiver for their transactions to be positive. If caregivers are abusive, maladaptive transactions occur and negatively affect the children's personalities. When these children become adults, they are likely to perpetuate the maladaptive transactions between themselves and their own offspring. In addition, reciprocal transactions between all of the family members and other individuals in their social environments influence their behaviors and feelings. Aspects of this social environment also influence the transactions, such as child-rearing practices, education, and the number of social supports (Anastasiow & Nucci, 1994).

The Family Systems Theory

The *family systems theory* is similar to the transactional theory in its perspective that the family is a system in which no one family member operates in isolation from the other members. The reciprocal nature of family interactions is such that whatever one person does affects the other members. This theory assumes that 1) the family is greater than the sum of its parts; 2) one cannot understand family functioning by just reviewing one part; 3) the interactions between family members shape their behaviors; and, consequently, 4) the family can encourage adaptive or maladaptive behaviors (Cook, Tessier, & Klein, 1996). As children are developing, the well-functioning family provides for their basic needs, which builds the children's sense of trust in people. When the family is poorly functioning and maltreating their children, however, the sense of trust is not developed. The children often live in fear, mistrust others, and exhibit difficulties in their relationships with others (Barnett, 1997; Sameroff, 1995). The family systems theory thus takes into account the perspective of each family member as well as the behavior of the family unit as a whole. In order to help students who are maltreated, teachers need to work on improving the interactions in the child's family system (Lambie, 2000).

CAUSES OF CHILD MALTREATMENT

These theories have many similarities and some differences, but a common assumption in all of them is that no one cause or risk factor is responsible for maltreatment. Instead, child abuse and neglect is the result of complex, multiple interactions among risk and protective factors. When the risk factors exceed the protective factors or when the stressors in the family overwhelm its resources, maltreatment can occur. Therefore, the interactions of multiple stressors can predict maltreatment rather than just one risk factor (Barnett, 1997; Master & Coatsworth, 1995; Sameroff & Chandler, 1975). In addition, the well-being of children depends on the number of protective factors in their environments (Sameroff, 1995). Risk factors are discussed in the following section. Protective factors are described later in the chapter. Risk factors can occur within the environment, the family, the caregiver, and the child.

Risk Factors in the Environment

Environmental risk factors include social ills, such as chronic unemployment, poverty, homelessness, social isolation, living in a crime-ridden neighborhood, and the acceptance of violence as a cultural norm in the community. Although the majority of families reported for maltreatment do come from impoverished backgrounds, it is essential not to stereotype families. Maltreatment can and does occur in families of all socioeconomic levels. One reason that there appears to be a close association between poverty and maltreatment is that wealthy abusive families tend to be underreported, whereas poor families tend to be overreported (Sattler, 1998). A number of reporting professionals may not believe that respected upper-class families would abuse or neglect their children. Not considering abuse just because a family appears friendly, highly educated, or wealthy can contribute to child morbidity and mortality as a result of undiscovered maltreatment (Christian, 1999).

Additional risk factors for low-income families may have emerged from federal and state policies on welfare reforms. Cuts were made in welfare funds to encourage the recipients to go to work. Because of their lack of training, however, many family members obtained entry-level positions that did not raise their incomes above poverty level. Another risk factor is the increase in homelessness. Because of inadequate finances, a number of families are forced to live in temporary shelters that lack privacy, have high noise levels, and provide few opportunities for nurturing parent–child interactions. Both caregivers and children become frustrated and angry because their basic needs for food, permanent shelter, clothing, safety, and nurturance are unmet. These multiple stressors can sometimes interact or compound and increase the potential for child maltreatment.

Risk Factors in Families

Teachers should be aware of risk factors within the families of their students in addition to risk factors in the environment. A striking characteristic of many families that are at risk is the family's isolation from social supports, such as assistance from extended family, friends, neighbors, and community helpers. Other risk factors in families are domestic violence, marital discord, harsh discipline, support of corporal punishment, unrealistic expectations of children, a family with multiple children who are very close together in age, and single teenage parents who may lack the maturity to adequately nurture their offspring (Lowenthal & Lowenthal, 1997; Reppucci, Britner, & Woolard, 1997).

Risk Factors in Caregivers

There are a number of risk factors in the parents or caregivers. One of the most common is a family history of maltreatment as children. Some studies suggest that as many as 70% of parents who abuse children were neglected or abused in their childhood (Egeland, 1998; Milner & Chilamkurti, 1991). A review of these studies concluded that other risk factors for parents or caregivers included depression; substance abuse; the tendency to blame others for the maltreatment; negative and angry feelings about their children; a history of family violence; limited knowledge about child development; and the use of punitive, harsh discipline (Milner & Chilamburti, 1993).

The personalities of these caregivers can be predictive of child maltreatment and inadequate parenting skills. Caregivers who have explosive personalities tend to anger easily at the misbehaviors of their children, which then leads to abuse. These caregivers may have unrealistic expectations of their children. When these expectations are not met, they blame the children and maltreat them. Caregivers who are abusive often are egocentric in their perspectives about parenting practices. Nurturing caregiving requires empathy and the ability to care for a dependent child. These abilities depend on the capacity of the caregivers to see another person's point of view, a skill that egocentric individuals lack.

Risk Factors in Children

Children with disabilities are especially vulnerable to the maltreatment of their caregivers. A report by the National Center on Child Abuse and Neglect (NCCAN; 1996) reviewed information about the number of children with disabilities who are maltreated. In a sample of 1,000 children who were maltreated, 36 had disabilities. A child with a disability is 1.7 times more likely to be abused than a child without a disability (NCCAN, 1996). The rate for emotional abuse in children with disabilities is 2.8 times higher than that for children without disabilities. Children with mental retardation appear to be most at risk for sexual abuse (Christian, 1999). Neglect of children with disabilities also is a growing concern, as a lack of basic care can impede their progress and compound their impairments (Christian, 1999). Reasons for the particular vulnerability of children with disabilities may be attributed to the following:

1. They are more dependent on caregivers to meet their basic needs.
2. They have infrequent contact with their peers, especially when physical disabilities prevent their mobility.
3. They have difficulties with impulsivity, reasoning, and problem solving.
4. They have difficulties in predicting the consequences of their behaviors.
5. They often experience rejection from others, which increases their need for affection and extra attention from the caregivers.
6. They have limited understanding about sex and sexual advances.

7.   They have innocent beliefs that all people have good intentions and would not take advantage of them (Carmody, 1991; Sattler, 1998).

Another interpretation of this vulnerability to maltreatment is that it is not the disability itself that causes the child abuse or neglect but rather the interactions of the accompanying stressors (Ammerman, Lubetsky, & Drudy, 1991). These stressors can include the increased cost of rearing children with disabilities, the extra burdens of caring for the children, the possible increase in their behavior problems, their limited adaptive or functional skills, and family members' negative attitudes about disabilities.

Other characteristics may account for their vulnerability to maltreatment, such as premature birth with medical complications, low birth weight, chronic illness, hyperactivity, noncompliant and violent behaviors, difficult temperament, aggression, and difficulty in interpreting the body language of angry caregivers. It is important to note, however, that children are not to blame for their maltreatment and that it is inappropriate for caregivers to condone it (Gootman, 1993; Sobsey, 1994).

PROFILES OF OFFENDERS

In addition to the risk factors, teachers' knowledge of offenders' profiles or characteristics will assist them in the identification process. These profiles have been developed by researchers according to the type of abuse or neglect. The profiles consist of general characteristics, which will not apply to every offender.

Profile of the Sexual Offender

The profile of the sexual offender can include the following characteristics: a lack of assertiveness and social skills; excessive hostility; a lack of intimacy with an equal; a manipulative personality, which can be used to trick the child into performing sexual activities; inadequate cognitive processing skills, such as confusing sex with love or rationalizing that the child wanted sex; failure to bond with the child victim; loneliness; a childhood history of sexual maltreatment; and substance abuse, which breaks down normal inhibitions (Becker, 1994; Roundy & Horton, 1991; Sattler, 1998).

Profile of the Physical Abuser

The profile of the physically abusive offender consists of the following characteristics: isolation from social supports; multiple stressors, such as financial and medical problems; marital conflicts with submissive–dominant relationships; a history of domestic violence; belief in harsh, punitive discipline and in corporal punishment; the necessity to control each family member; poor impulse control, emotional self-regulation, and ability to cope; antisocial personality traits; and inappropriate expectations of children (Sattler, 1998).

Profile of the Psychological Abuser

As mentioned previously, psychological abuse has been linked to all types of maltreatment, but it is especially linked to physical abuse and neglect. Therefore, the characteristics of this type of offender can and do overlap with the other profiles of caregivers who are abusive and neglectful. Unfortunately, the majority of these caregivers are the parents of the children who are abused. They can come from all income levels, but the cases involving offenders who have significant financial resources are underreported as they often enter the mental health system instead of the law enforcement system (Crittenden, 1996; Sattler, 1998). Psychologically abusive caregivers seek control over their children. To obtain this control, the offenders will belittle and demean the victims. These abusers will not realize or will not be concerned about the negative effects that this type of verbal abuse has on the self-confidence and self-esteem of their children (Crittenden, 1996).

Profile of the Neglectful Offender

The profile of the neglectful offender consists of characteristics such as poverty, lack of social services, psychological immaturity due to a childhood history of neglect, distrust in people, shallow personal relationships, social withdrawal, limited knowledge about the needs of children, and inadequate parenting skills. In addition, these offenders often are apathetic about improving their lives, tend to escape from problems, and have unrealistic goals for themselves and their children (Gaudin, 1993).

THE CONCEPT OF RESILIENCY

The concept of resiliency can provide teachers with suggestions about how they can reduce risk factors and make a positive difference in the lives of children in their classes who are maltreated. *Resiliency* has been defined as the ability to spring back from the adversity associated with risk factors (Bender, Rosenkrans, & Crane, 1999). Just as the possibility of poor outcomes increases with multiple risk factors, the probability of favorable outcomes increases with an array of protective factors that provide resiliency (Christian, 1999). Identifying these protective factors can lead teachers to appropriate school interventions that build resiliency in students who are at risk. The protective factors lie within the children, their families, and the community.

Protective Factors in Children

Resilient children tend to have personalities and temperament qualities that elicit positive responses from other people (Young-Eisendrath, 1996). Resilient infants have been described by caregivers as active, affectionate, alert, responsive, and good-natured. Preschoolers who are resilient are reported to be self-confident, independent, and sociable. School-age resilient children are cooperative, competent, goal-oriented in their play, enjoy challenging experiences, have good problem-solving and coping skills, achieve success in school, and communicate well with peers and adults. Their outlook on life is positive and optimistic about the future. Their resiliency provides them with an inner sense of control in which they attribute success to their own efforts and not to luck or other people. Therefore, children who are resilient do not blame others for their failures. These children reach out to adults when assistance is needed, and their engaging personalities encourage positive responses (Werner, 1995).

At adolescence, resilient youth have clear long-term goals and are more mature and responsible than many of their peers. In order to escape from their unpleasant home environments, they often participate in extracurricular activities, such as art, music, drama, and sports. These activities deter them from substance abuse and delinquent behaviors. Many are leaders among their peers because of their sociability, empathy, competence, and sense of humor. Resilient adolescents have a remarkable insight about their negative home lives, and, if necessary, they maintain an emotional distance from their abusers. These resilient teenagers are successful against adversity and can teach us, as educators, how to meet life's challenges with confidence and hope (Young-Eisendrath, 1996).

Protective Factors in Families

Protective factors that encourage resiliency in families are stability, cooperative spouses, respect for family members, healthy and well-groomed children, and strong parent–child relationships. If parents are not available, alternative family members, such as grandparents and older siblings, can provide the necessary care and nurturance for attachment and bonding to occur. These family members build a sense of trust in the children that is essential for healthy relationships later in life. Several studies indicate that the love and consistent support of grandparents during early childhood can predict emotional health for children at risk for maltreatment by their parents (Katz, 1997; Werner, 1990). In addition, caregiving from nurturing older siblings is a protective factor that buffers stress at home for children at risk. These relationships are as close as those between supportive parents and their offspring.

Protective Factors in the Community

Alternate caregivers, who may be found in the community, include friends, neighbors, clergy, health care personnel, and teachers. These individuals take a special interest in helping and responding to the needs of children who are maltreated. In this role, teachers can make a positive difference for children who are at risk by creating a school environment that is safe and supportive. This type of environment serves as a refuge from abuse and neglect at home. Teachers can provide warmth, be caring, have empathy, create predictable routines, provide consistent rules, maintain clear structure, and, most important, be positive role models for children who lack these things at home (Katz, 1997). Resilient students tend to like school and are successful there. When they become adults, many tell stories about how their favorite teachers inspired them and made them feel confident of success. Resilient students want their teachers to be respectful, caring, encouraging, and available when needed. As educators, teachers can build resiliency by incorporating these characteristics into a curricula that emphasizes competence, belonging, usefulness, and optimism (Sagor, 1996). Lambie (2000) and McMillan and Reed (1993) provided some other suggestions for teachers on how to foster resiliency:

1. Teachers should provide support for the children and family members who are at risk and should assist them in gaining access to needed services in the community.
2. Teachers should instruct students in basic social skills by modeling and reinforcing positive behaviors. Teachers should encourage cooperation and friendships among the children.
3. Teachers should teach problem solving and ways of coping with stress so that students can better solve their difficulties.
4. Teachers should give the students classroom responsibilities, such as useful jobs. They should encourage them to help younger children. These actions improve self-image and confidence.

5. Most important, teachers should be positive mentors for the students. They are the ones who can show the children that they can be successful at school.

CONCLUSION

In this chapter, theories and causes of child maltreatment as well as risk factors and the concept of resiliency have been described. Chapter 3 discusses the possible effects of abuse and neglect on the development and school performance of children who have been maltreated.

3

EFFECTS OF MALTREATMENT ON DEVELOPMENT AND SCHOOL PERFORMANCE

In this chapter, the possible effects of maltreatment on the development of children from early childhood through adolescence are discussed. The neurological, psychological, social, linguistic, adaptive, and motor difficulties are described. Then there is a discussion of the impact of maltreatment on cognition, learning, and school performance. Because of the sharp increase of child maltreatment in the United States, a teacher is very likely to have at least one child in his or her classroom who is abused and neglected. Therefore, to intervene most effectively for these students, it is imperative to understand the possible effects of abuse on children's development and ability to learn.

NEUROLOGICAL EFFECTS OF ABUSE AND NEGLECT

Since the 1990s, research has increasingly focused on providing more information about the results of maltreatment on the neurology and development of the brain during the first years of life (Perry, Pollard, Blakely, Baker, & Vigilante, 1995). At birth, the brain is the most immature organ in the human body and will continue to develop as a result of nature or genetics and through environmental experiences. Environmental experiences can be positive or negative for healthy development (Terr, 1991). Different areas of the brain are responsible for specific functions. Systems in the frontal area are responsible for abstract thought. Systems in the limbic area regulate affect, emotion, and the attachment process. Other systems in the brain stem regulate the heart rate, blood pressure, and states of arousal (Perry et al., 1995).

In these diverse areas of the brain, there are millions of nerve cells or neurons that are connected to each other by synapses. The synapses are pathways that compose the wiring of the brain (Newberger, 1997). The wiring allows the various regions of the brain to communicate with each other. Brain development after birth consists of a continuous process of wiring the connections between neurons. New synapses form, and others that are not being used are pruned or broken away. During the first year of life, a baby can have an amazing array of 1,000 trillion synapses in his or her brain. By the age of 10, however, the pruning or weeding-out process occurs more frequently than the formation of synapses (Nash, 1997). The child then has about 500 trillion synapses, which is approximately the same number as an adult.

Neurodevelopment can be disrupted in the young child in two ways: The first way is by a lack of sensory experiences during critical processes of brain development. Sensory experiences are necessary for the optimal organization of the brain (Stermer, 1997). The second way is through an abnormal activation of neuron patterns caused by extremely negative experiences, such as maltreatment and neglect (Perry, 1993). These atypical environmental events can result in the malfunctioning of the regions of the brain responsible for the regulation of affect, empathy, and emotions. Continual abuse and neglect also can cause a disruption in the attachment process of young children with their caregivers and a lack of trust in their environments (Nash, 1997).

The neurological reasons for the malfunctioning of the brain can be traced to the initial responses to threat that human beings exhibit (LeDoux, 1992). This reaction often is called the *fight or flight response*, which prepares individuals to defend themselves against perceived threats. Under the stress of the fight or flight response, the body exhibits an increase in the heart rate and in the production of a steroid hormone called *cortisol*. High levels of cortisol cause the death of brain cells and a reduction of the number of synapses. Studies of adults who have experienced continuous abuse as young children indicate that the prolonged stress of maltreatment results in a shrinkage of the regions of the brain that are responsible for memory, learning, and the regulations of affect and emotional expression (Newberger, 1997). Other studies have shown that the brains of children who are maltreated can be 20%–30% smaller when compared with those of their peers who have not been maltreated (Perry, 1993). It appears that the maltreatment could have caused parts of their brains to waste away.

Children who are maltreated tend to develop brains that are attuned to dangers. At the slightest threat, the children will anxiously track any signs that indicate further abusive attacks. These early experiences of stress form templates in the brain in which the fear responses become fixed. The brain becomes organized for survival and leaves these children constantly in states of high alert, which could help them to avoid further maltreatment but could jeopardize their optimal development. The children are at great risk for emotional, behavior, learning, and physical difficulties (Herman, 1992; Terr, 1990). Other long-term effects could be the reduction in the opportunities for comfort, support, and nurturing, which are necessary for secure relationships.

Other ways of coping with fears of maltreatment are freezing and disassociative responses, which can be exhibited by infants, toddlers, and preschoolers. Physical flight often is not possible for very young children. The freezing or lack of movement response occurs when the children perceive that they have no control over threatening events. The freezing response allows time to process and evaluate the stress-producing experience. Abusive caregivers, however, often interpret this reaction as noncompliance and then further mistreat the children. If the maltreatment is of sufficient duration, the organization of the brain again is altered. The template of fear becomes fixed in the brain, and the children consistently feel anxious and frustrated even when experiences are nonthreatening. The children's brains seem to react with continuous symptoms of fear. Behaviors that can result from these feelings are irritability, loss of sleep, hypervigilance, hyperactivity, aggression, tantrums, and regression in development (James, 1994).

Disassociation is another response to maltreatment. It is a response in which individuals separate their painful experiences from conscious awareness. The use of disassociation protects children from overwhelming emotions and thoughts about the maltreatment. When carried to an extreme, however, this response can result in memory disorders, amnesia, and hallucinations (Herman, 1992; Terr, 1991). The children also may exhibit personality and self-identity disorders.

PSYCHOLOGICAL EFFECTS OF ABUSE AND NEGLECT

Psychological effects of abuse and neglect include the deregulation of affect, the avoidance of intimacy, provocative behaviors, and disturbances in the attachment process.

Deregulation of Affect

Children who are maltreated often display difficulties in their regulation of affect and emotions. They frequently have intrusive and intense emotional memories of their maltreatment, which they attempt to control by denying and avoiding displays of their feelings (Brooks & Rice, 1997). Sometimes, the only way they can identify their emotions is through physiological responses, such as increased heart rate and perspiration. The children appear capable of describing the feelings of other people but cannot describe their own feelings.

Avoidance of Intimacy

Children who have been maltreated tend to avoid intimacy in their relationships as they get older because the feeling of closeness increases their vulnerability and lack of control (James, 1994). Intimacy is not welcome because it represents a threat rather than nurturance and love. To avoid intimacy, children may exhibit withdrawal, lack of eye contact, hyperactivity, and inappropriate behaviors.

Provocative Behaviors

If children who are maltreated are unable to experience relief through disassociation, they may exhibit more provocative behaviors in order to initiate the numbing response that can quiet their fears of more maltreatment. Some of these provocative behaviors include aggression and inflicting harm to others; inflicting harm to themselves, such as self-mutilation and suicide; and behaving in antisocial ways, which bring them harsh punishments. The underlying purpose behind these provocative and emotional acts is to produce the numbing responses that can lessen their extreme anxiety. It also appears that in childhood, boys who are maltreated display externalizing disorders (e.g., attention-deficit/hyperactivity disorder, conduct difficulties, and oppositional-defiant disorders) more than girls (Perry et al., 1995). Girls who are maltreated, however, have internalizing disorders, such as depression, anxiety, and fears. Both sexes are at risk for medical problems, such as asthma, heart disease, allergies, and immune system disorders (Perry, 1996).

Disturbances in the Attachment Process

Attachment is viewed by Hanson and Lynch (1995) as the bond that young children form with their primary caregivers, usually their parents. Theories of the attachment process provide information about the role of early relationships in shaping the development of the child's personality and socioemotional adjustment (Kemp, 1998; Morrison et al., 1999). The attachment process is important because it affects the children's abilities to cope with stress, regulate emotions, benefit from social supports, and form nurturing and loving relationships. All of these abilities become problematic for children who are maltreated because their attachment processes are disrupted (Barnett, 1997). Under typical circumstances, the caregivers and the infants form close emotional bonds and secure relationships. Attachments can be observed in the following behaviors of infants and their caregivers or parents: The infants demonstrate strong preferences for their primary caregivers and derive enjoyment and comfort from that closeness with them, and the caregivers show their attachments in their desire to nurture, comfort, protect, and enjoy the infants while demonstrating uneasiness and sadness when separated. Because the attachment process promotes feelings of security, trust, and self-esteem, it also furthers the infants' desires to explore and learn from their environments.

Secure attachments help children in all areas of development but are essential in establishing their feelings of self-identify and worth (Moroz, 1996). The experiences of abuse and neglect can impede the attachment process and diminish the children's feelings of security and trust in their caregivers. Because of the maltreatment, children feel unworthy, unloved, and view the world as a dangerous place. Their motivation for learning and exploring their environment is diminished because their energy is focused on being hypervigilant to guard against further abuse. When their caregivers are neglectful, uncaring, and abusive, children become more vulnerable to the stressors of life and will have difficulties in forming intimate and positive relationships with others. The unmet needs of children who are maltreated result in anger and resentment toward their caregivers, which then transfer to other relationships in their lives (Zeanah, 1993). Their difficulties in self-regulating their emotions also place them at great risk for later behavior problems (Moroz, 1993).

SOCIAL EFFECTS OF ABUSE AND NEGLECT

In addition to psychological difficulties, child maltreatment can have detrimental effects on social adjustment. Results of a number of studies indicate these problems in social development (Dodge, Pettit, & Bates, 1994). In one investigation, for example, the single area that most discriminated students who were maltreated from their peers who were not maltreated was social acceptance (Vondra,

Barnett, & Cicchetti, 1990). The educators in this study believed that the lack of social competence was detrimental to school behaviors and academic performance. In their ratings, the teachers perceived that the students who were maltreated had fewer social skills when compared with their peers who were not maltreated.

Conclusions from a review of a number of studies concurred with this view of the social incompetence of children who are abused and neglected. In their interactions with peers who are not abused, these children consistently demonstrated more aggression, less prosocial behaviors, and more inappropriate reactions to peer distress or emotional upsets (Barnett, 1997; Cooney, 1991; Youngblade & Belsky, 1989). These students were more likely to avoid or ignore prosocial initiations of play with their same-age peers and resisted overtures of friendship. They also responded to their classmates who were in trouble or hurt with fear and rejection in contrast to students' typical responses of sympathy, concern, and offers to help. It appeared that instead of trying to assist their fellow classmates, the students who were maltreated became angry, hostile, and aggressive. According to Youngblade and Belsky (1989), one reason for these unusual behaviors could be the negative modeling by caregivers when their children were in distress. The children who were maltreated also were more likely to avoid appropriate relationships with their teachers or other people who had not mistreated them. Apparently, their lack of quality relationships at home became replicated at school because of their fears of abuse in close friendships.

According to Cooney (1991), another social difficulty for some of these students was their fear of specific people or places that brought back memories of the trauma suffered at home. These children exhibited extreme withdrawal, agitation, or panic and became loners who disliked social contacts. If they were absent from school, many of their classmates did not even notice or ask about them. For other students who were maltreated, the opposite occurred. They threatened their peers and made derogatory comments about them. Thus, they modeled and repeated the actions of their caregivers who were abusive. If the children who are abused were scapegoats at home, they often tried to make scapegoats of younger, more vulnerable students. Unfortunately, the children who were maltreated were very skilled at alienating their peers because they were consistently taught this at home. Instead of feeling complimented when praised, they reacted with suspicion and hostility.

Other social problems for students who are maltreated could arise from a sense of inferiority, low self-esteem, a feeling of being unworthy of friends, and a lack of self-confidence. Studies by Briere and Runtz (1993) indicated that there is a very strong relationship between severe psychological abuse and low self-esteem. Results suggested that the social functioning of children who were psychologically abused was the poorest compared with all types of abuse. Their sense of inferiority made them reluctant to volunteer in class or participate in extracurricular activities (Briere & Runtz, 1993). As adolescents, children who were maltreated tried to be "hidden" students to avoid calling attention to themselves. Role confusion, loneliness, and self-identity difficulties were common. Some of these teenagers constantly looked for reassurance and would do anything that pleased their teachers or other adults. Others would make friends with teenagers who were abused and neglected as well, who demonstrated hostility toward others, who were likely to become troublemakers, who became destructive, and who used violence as their way to solve social difficulties. Several theorists have suggested that healthy peer relationships promote the development of moral reasoning, reciprocity, and cooperation (Erikson, 1968; Vygotsky, 1978). Antisocial relationships and the lack of intimacy at adolescence and in adulthood were predicted when students who were maltreated lacked satisfying friendships because of either withdrawal or aggression (Briere & Runtz, 1993; Dodge et al., 1994).

All types of child maltreatment can lead to unusual and worrisome behaviors and feelings, such as extreme unhappiness; hatred of others; emotional instability; depression; excessive fears; suicidal thoughts; and psychosomatic symptoms, such as lack of appetite, sleep disorders, and illnesses. The more severe the abuse or neglect, the more these feelings and behaviors can multiply. When children or adolescents demonstrated these disorders in their relationships, they were likely to be rejected by their peers and did not benefit from the appropriate peer modeling of close friendships and positive social skills (Manly, Cicchetti, & Barnett, 1994).

EFFECTS ON MOTOR DEVELOPMENT AND ADAPTIVE SKILLS

Both fine and gross motor abilities, as well as adaptive or self-help skills, can be compromised when children are maltreated. A number of children who are maltreated are malnourished, which causes lethargy, weakness, and the inability to use the large muscles in an age-appropriate manner. Their gross motor coordination is diminished with weight loss and may result in stunted rates of growth (Skuse, Reilly, & Wolke, 1994). Some studies indicate that there is a corresponding lack of activity with delays in physical exploration and learning from the environment (England & Sundberg, 1996).

Young children who are severely physically abused, such as those who have shaken baby syndrome, develop neurological damage that can include cerebral palsy; traumatic brain injuries; and difficulties in vision, hearing, and speech. Untreated bone fractures from physical abuse can result in bone and joint malignments with a corresponding reduction in gross and fine motor skills. An investigation by Halfon, Mendonca, and Berkowitz (1995) suggested that about two thirds of children younger than 7 years of age who were maltreated demonstrated neuromuscular delays and problems with fine motor coordination. Lack of supervision and medical neglect can contribute to motor problems. The lack of supervision by caregivers who are neglectful places the child at risk for accidents, such as injuries from falls and burns from fires. Both types of injuries can cause motor impairments. Medical neglect, such as in untreated illnesses, also may result in motor coordination disorders. Finally, fine motor skills will be delayed in children if they are deprived of relevant stimulation and experiences, such as coloring, painting, cutting, pasting, working puzzles, manipulating toys, and building with small blocks, by parents who are neglectful.

Along with coordination difficulties, adaptive abilities necessary for daily living may not adequately develop when children are neglected or abused. Skills in self-care and community living can regress when children are consistently maltreated because neglectful or abusive caregivers may not model or reinforce these skills (Briere & Elliot, 1994). Health care specialists in eating disorders are interested in the possible relationships between sexual and physical abuse and bulimia (episodes of binge eating and vomiting) as well as anorexia (lack of appetite, refusal to eat based on abnormal psychological reasons). These eating disorders can be methods of coping with the emotional upsets caused by the maltreatment because they act as self-soothing distractions from non-food–related anxieties (Briere & Elliot, 1994).

Sleeping, waking, and toileting routines also may be disrupted because of the children's acute fears, hypervigilance, and feelings of vulnerability for further maltreatment if they are not always alert. Yet according to some research, the adaptive functioning of some children who were maltreated appeared to be normal when compared with their peers who were not maltreated (Barnett, 1997). One reason for this apparent contradiction is that the children who were maltreated learned survival and self-help skills because of the lack of care in their homes. A second reason could be that the caregivers who were abusive demanded compliance and independence in daily living skills (Barnett, 1997).

EFFECTS ON COMMUNICATION AND LANGUAGE DEVELOPMENT

In many instances, maltreatment has serious adverse effects on communication and language development. A number of children with socioemotional problems caused by maltreatment have coexisting language delays and impairments (Windsor, 1995). The presence of maltreatment seems to correlate with language disorders. The reason for this correlation is related to the concept of *social competence,* which is defined as the effectiveness of interpersonal relationships (Gallagher, 1991; Guralnick, 1992). Not only does language occur in social situations and interactions, but the appropriate use of language itself also is considered a social skill. In a relevant study by Mack and Warr-Leeper (1992), the performance of 20 adolescents who were maltreated was compared on a battery of language tests with that of a comparison group of peers who were not maltreated but who had similar socioeconomic backgrounds. Seventeen of the twenty teenagers who were maltreated were diagnosed with speech-language delays and impairments. In addition, according to Gallagher (1991), the rate of occurrence of these disorders was approximately 10 times higher in the group of adolescents who were abused and neglected than in their peers who were not maltreated.

These language and communication delays, however, do not begin in adolescence. There is strong evidence that these impairments start at a very early age. Several studies have indicated that from birth to 2 years of age, infants and toddlers who were maltreated primarily expressed their needs by whining and crying instead of by using gestures and sounds (Rivers & Hedrick, 1998). Nonverbal communication skills, such as meaningful facial expressions, body language, and turn taking, also were depressed. Preschoolers between the ages of 2 and 5 who were maltreated frequently displayed restricted vocabulary, delays in articulation, inappropriate word usage, reduced length of utterances, difficulties in formulating organized sentences, and depressed pragmatic skills or language use in social situations when compared with their peers who were not maltreated (Amster, 1999). On average, children who were abused and neglected displayed language delays ranging from 6 to 9 months. They tended to use nouns more often than age-appropriate verb tenses, pronouns, and prepositions. In addition, these children used more repetitions in their verbalizations, which then were less informative in comparison with their classmates who were not maltreated (Amster, 1999).

At 6 years of age and older, other delays were found in the maltreated children's receptive and expressive vocabularies, semantic abilities, syntax skills, the formulation of meaningful sentences, and pragmatics. Reasons for these delays in language development were thought to include the following: In early childhood, when there was a window of opportunity for language development, children who were abused and neglected by their caregivers demonstrated less playfulness, turn taking, and verbal interactions than their peers who were not maltreated (Eckenrode, Laird, & Doris, 1993). Neglect appeared to have the most deleterious effect on language development in comparison with other types of maltreatment. The reason for this was that chronic neglect resulted in a lack of interaction between children and their caregivers. Therefore, there was a paucity of verbal stimulation and linguistic opportunities for the children to use language to meet their needs. Caregivers who were abusive, as opposed to caregivers who were neglectful, interacted more, even if negatively, with their children, which gave the children more chances for their language skills to develop.

In one study, the lack of interaction was observed in some adolescent mothers who were neglectful, who infrequently verbalized with their children, who in turn responded very little to them (Osofsky, Hann, & Peebles, 1993). When the mothers did talk, they tended to use short, terse commands rather than make use of more elaborate language. Results of another study of the language comprehension abilities of school-age children who were neglected concurred with the conclusion that the lack of opportunities for verbal interactions appeared to be the most important cause of their language impairments (Kurtz, Jaudin, Wodarski, & Howling, 1993). In addition to neglect, physical abuse was found in another investigation to depress language performance because these children were socialized by their caregivers who were abusive to respond either in short utterances or not at all. This was done to demonstrate their compliance and avoid further abuse (Amster, 1999). Conversational skills were discouraged because when the children tried to verbalize, they were belittled, criticized, and told to be quiet. The children found it safer and not as threatening to remain silent. They then lacked opportunities to verbalize their feelings coherently and were unable to use abstract language, which is important in the upper grades for school success. Their conversation also was mostly limited to the present or the here and now with few references to past or future events (Amster, 1999).

Another detriment to school performance is the lack of an adequate oral language foundation for the written language skills of reading, spelling, written expression, and story problems in mathematics. A number of studies have indicated that the verbal IQ scores of children who are maltreated are significantly lower than their nonverbal intelligence (Coster & Cicchetti, 1993; Snyder, Nathanson, & Saywitz, 1993). A disturbing relationship found in some of these investigations is the link between adolescents' violent and aggressive behaviors and inadequate school performances. Because of their low self-confidence and anger caused by maltreatment, the adolescents felt incompetent and unmotivated to succeed in school. Their subsequent academic failures led them to act out their frustration by using violence as a method of solving their emotional difficulties (Coster & Cicchetti, 1993; Snyder, Nathanson, & Saywitz, 1993). Teachers need to recognize the possible reciprocal relationships between child maltreatment, emotional disorders, inadequate language development, and lack of school success so that they can plan appropriate school interventions, which foster linguistic and academic competence in children who are maltreated.

EFFECTS ON COGNITION, LEARNING, AND SCHOOL PERFORMANCE

Teachers have a prevailing interest in the learning abilities of their students. It is important for them to consider the cognitive implications of child maltreatment, which include difficulties in learning and in academic performance at school. Many studies have consistently emphasized that children who are abused or neglected on average score lower on cognitive measures, demonstrate poorer school achievement, and earn lower grades when compared with their peers of similar socioeconomic backgrounds who are not abused (Barnett, 1997; Vondra et al., 1990). These students appeared to have delays in the motivational and behavioral aspects of cognitive functioning and did not enjoy challenging academic tasks because of their fears of failure.

Since the 1990s, theory on child–caregiver attachment has proposed that underlying emotional problems caused by negative interactions between a child and his or her caregiver may account for some of this poor school performance (Barnett, Vondra, & Shonk, 1996; Vondra et al., 1990). Children with caring parents or caregivers learn to view themselves as worthy, lovable, and competent in school-related and cognitive tasks. Children who have caregivers who are insensitive, however, may see themselves as unworthy of love or caring and incompetent in academic performance. The detrimental characteristics of abusive parenting often lead to a loss of self-esteem and a lack of motivation to achieve at school. As a result, these children are inattentive and try to avoid academic work.

At a very early age, children who are maltreated exhibit low self-esteem, behavior difficulties, and difficulties in adapting to their child care and preschool environments. Toddlers who are abused respond more negatively to their mirror images and make fewer positive statements about themselves than do their peers who are not abused (Beeghly & Cicchetti, 1994). In addition, toddlers who are maltreated often display more aggressive behaviors than their peers who are not maltreated. These aggressive behaviors include hitting, kicking, biting, and unprovoked hostility. These behaviors may reflect the children's inner rage about the maltreatment and an inability to self-regulate their emotions in socially acceptable ways. It appears that by preschool age, specific behaviors are associated with the different types of abuse.

In a study by Erickson, Stroufe, and Pianta (1989), preschoolers who were physically abused exhibited more hostile and noncompliant behavior than their peers from similar socioeconomic backgrounds who were not abused. The children who were maltreated also were more impulsive, disorganized, and less successful on preacademic tasks. They lacked the necessary social, work, and readiness skills for age-appropriate adjustment in their preschool and kindergarten classes. These skills were not taught or modeled by their caregivers who were abusive at home. Almost half of the children who were physically abused were referred for special education or retention by the end of their kindergarten year. At school age, they continued to have severe academic problems, especially in language, math, and reading, and were more likely to repeat grades (Erickson et al., 1989). Similarly, young children who were emotionally abused displayed more disruptive, noncompliant behavior and a lack of persistence in their school work when compared with their peers who were not abused. These young children had to have explicit directions and direct teacher supervision to complete their assignments. They also displayed a lack of creativity and enthusiasm for learning when compared with children from similar socioeconomic backgrounds who were not maltreated.

Patterns of behavior that were characteristic of the students who were sexually abused in the study by Erickson et al. (1989) included extreme anxiety, fear of failure, depression, hopelessness, inattentiveness, and difficulties in following directions. Their social behaviors ranged from withdrawal to extreme aggression, with the consequence of rejection by their classmates. Other common characteristics of these children were their dependency on adults and their strong needs for the affection and approval of their teachers. Their dependent behaviors seemed to be reflective of their roles as victims at home. Another study by Briere and Elliot (1994) also concluded that the long-term effects of sexual abuse were social, behavior, and academic difficulties. The students who were sexually abused, in comparison with other students who were not maltreated, were more likely to be placed in classes for children with emotional disabilities (Briere & Elliot, 1994).

In a number of investigations, the group of children who were neglected appeared to display the most severe problems (Eckenrode et al., 1993; Mash & Wolfe, 1991). These children were the least successful on cognitive tasks in kindergarten and primary grades when compared with other children who suffered from other forms of abuse or maltreatment. They also were more anxious, inattentive, and apathetic and had difficulty in concentrating on academic tasks. Socially, they exhibited inappropriate behaviors and were not accepted by their peers. These young children rarely displayed positive affect, humor, or enjoyment. A majority of children who were neglected were retained or referred for special education (due to learning disabilities, developmental delays, or socioemotional difficulties) at the end of kindergarten. A major reason for these children's poor performances could have been the lack of stimulation that the children received in their homes due to poor quality and chaotic living conditions. The parents or caregivers who were neglectful presented direct threats to their children's school performance. Low educational aspirations and the lack of encouragement of learning undermined the academic achievements of their children. The effects of their environments became more obvious at school age as these children lacked opportunities to learn the necessary social and academic skills for school success.

A number of studies have indicated that children between the ages of 6 and 12 years who were maltreated demonstrated more cognitive delays, attention-deficit/hyperactivity disorders, and learning disabilities and were considered more at risk for school failure and dropping out than their peers who were not maltreated (Kurtz et al., 1993; Reyome, 1993). The results also suggested that the children who were maltreated demonstrated more negative affect toward their teachers and were less motivated to learn than the children who were not maltreated. The children who were physically abused had lower self-esteem and displayed more delays in cognitive problem solving. The children who were neglected were less compliant, more dependent, and withdrawn. The children who were psychologically abused were less persistent and enthusiastic in their academic work when compared with their peers who were not abused. All of the groups of children who were maltreated were rated by their teachers as being more impulsive, less flexible, more impatient, and tended to make more nonrelevant responses to questions than a comparison group of students who were not maltreated.

Other teacher ratings in these studies also suggested that the students who were abused were more overactive, less attentive, more aggressive, and more impulsive than their classmates who were not abused (Kurtz et al., 1993; Reyome, 1993). The teachers believed that they had to discipline these children frequently because of their lack of cooperation and limited social skills in the classroom. These children appeared less motivated to achieve at school and had difficulty learning. This common pattern of behaviors for different types of child abuse can reflect the fact that the different forms of abuse often overlap. Children may suffer from more than one type of abuse, such as a combination of emotional, sexual, and physical maltreatment.

Two more studies compared the different characteristics of children who were physically abused, sexually abused, or neglected (Eckenrode et al., 1993; Kurtz et al., 1993). The students who were physically abused displayed significant school problems. Their performance was poor in all academic subjects but particularly in the deductive reasoning necessary for success in mathematics and language. Their ability for abstract thought seemed to be directly linked to their underlying emotional problems, which interfered with their abilities to reason. They appeared to be underachievers and were more likely to be retained than their classmates who were not physically abused. In adolescence, these students were at risk for dropping out of school. LeDoux (1992) found that teachers and parents reported students who were physically abused as having significantly more behavior problems than their peers who were not abused.

Neglect was associated with the poorest academic achievement among the groups of students who were maltreated (Eckenrode et al., 1993; Kurtz et al., 1993; Mash & Wolfe, 1991). Teachers reported that these pupils were performing below grade level and that their rate of school absenteeism was nearly five times that of students in the comparison group who were not neglected. Neglect appears to have a greater long-term effect on academic performance than other forms of abuse. It also negatively affected these children's social skills and interactions as they engaged in less prosocial behaviors than children who experienced other types of abuse. Children who were sexually abused, however, were similar to children who were not abused in academic achievement and in the number of discipline problems. They did not significantly differ in any area of academic performance. Although sexual abuse has negative socioemotional consequences, its effects on academic achievement were not evident in these studies (Eckenrode et al., 1993; Kurtz et al., 1993). A number of studies did show that the effects of all abuse were most pronounced during the elementary and middle school grades. At adolescence, many of the children who were sexually abused dropped out so the effects diminished (Eckenrode et al., 1993; Kurtz et al., 1993). For all types of maltreatment, however, there is a compelling need for intervention by school personnel to try to prevent further abuse and neglect and to assist the children with their learning problems.

CONCLUSION

This chapter examined the possible effects of maltreatment on the development of children from early childhood through adolescence. Next, the impact of learning and school performance was reviewed. Chapter 4 examines the important role of teachers as mandated reporters of child maltreatment.

4

TEACHERS AS
MANDATED REPORTERS

A significant role of teachers in assisting children who have been maltreated is that of mandated reporters of suspected maltreatment. In this chapter, the reporting process for teachers is described. First, guidelines are provided for reporting, including relevant legislation, the meaning of the report as a request for an investigation, the personal liability of the teacher, and the information needed in the report. Next, recommendations are made about how to communicate and react to the child who is confiding in the teacher and how to communicate with the child's family members. Next, ethical concerns regarding privacy and confidentiality for the children and their families are described. Then, there is a discussion about the possible psychological consequences of the reporting process for the teachers, the children, the suspected offenders, and the families. In the last part of the chapter, the issues of appropriate feedback to the teachers about the results of the investigation and the need for teacher training are examined. As will be seen throughout this chapter, the role of the teacher as a reporter of suspected child maltreatment is both legally and ethically based.

GUIDELINES FOR REPORTING MALTREATMENT

Knowledge about the guidelines for making a report is essential for teachers as mandated reporters. The following information can assist educators.

Relevant Legislation

As mentioned in Chapter 1, all of the U.S. states have laws that require the reporting of suspected abuse or neglect of children (Coster
& Cicchetti, 1993). The legislation in each state defines the types
of abuse and neglect, designates the required reporters, explains
the reporting procedures, and describes the consequences for the failure to report suspected maltreatment. There are four categories of
professional, mandated reporters: 1) medical; 2) educational; 3) legal;
and; 4) human services professionals, such as social workers and therapists (Reppucci, Britner, & Woolard, 1997). In addition, all states allow anyone to report suspected maltreatment (Besharov, 1994). The
reporting laws have demonstrated their effectiveness by increasing
the number of reports. Results of studies indicate that in 1963, approximately 150,000 children were reported to be suspected victims
of abuse and neglect. In 1993, this number increased to approximately
3 million children (Besharov, 1994; McCurdy & Daro, 1994). Please
see Chapter 1 for a thorough discussion of the relevant legislation.

The Meaning of the Report

A *report* is a request for an investigation into a suspected cause of
maltreatment. The reporter is not required to *prove* that the abuse
or neglect is occurring. When teachers make the report, they are not
expected to complete the investigation. This is the responsibility of
the child protection and law enforcement agencies. Teachers just
need to have reasonable suspicions that maltreatment exists (Lowenthal, 1996). As educators, it is important to remember that mandated reporting is both a legal and an ethical responsibility. Failure
to report may result in criminal prosecution or other sanctions. The
criminal penalty could be similar to that of a misdemeanor, with
the fines ranging from $100 to $1,000 and a prison term of 5 days–
1 year (Besharov, 1994). In addition, the majority of states impose
civil liabilities for failures to report suspected maltreatment. These
sanctions, however, are rarely enforced.

Personal Liability of the Teacher

To encourage more reporting, legislation in all of the U.S. states
protects the teachers and other mandated reporters from personal liability if their reports are made in good faith. Twelve states have stip-
ulated criminal or civil penalties in their laws for making false,
malicious reports because of personal bias or prejudice (Sattler, 1998).
The protection against personal liability does not extend to acts of
perjury or to obtaining child testimony through threats or fraud.

In general, the state legislation requires the reporting of child maltreatment to child protection and law enforcement agencies within 24 hours. Teachers should be informed of their own state's definitions of child abuse and neglect and regulations for reporting. This information can be obtained by calling the telephone number listed under the Child Abuse heading in the local telephone directory. The National Child Abuse Hotline also can be contacted by calling their toll-free number, which is (800) 422-4453. Many school districts have set up their own policies that support their state's regulations. All educators should be aware of their school's policies.

The Information Needed in the Report

When a teacher makes a report to the child protection and law enforcement agencies, the following information is usually needed: the name of the child and family members, the child's address, the child's telephone number (if available), and the reasons for reporting. In some cases, additional information will be asked, such as whether any knowledge of previous maltreatment exists. The teacher may remain anonymous, but it will assist the agencies in substantiating the reports if they know the name of the caller (Nunnelley & Fields, 1999).

The Need for Training in the Reporting Process

There is a definite need to train teachers to report child maltreatment. The results of several studies indicated that teachers, when compared with other professionals, such as nurses and social workers, are the least informed and prepared to make reports of abuse or neglect (McIntyre, 1990). According to these studies, teachers are concerned about the maltreatment of their students but generally lack the information regarding how the state defines maltreatment as well as their states' reporting procedures. According to Besharov (1994), the most effective method of increasing the accuracy and quality of reports is better training of the mandated reporters. Some states have passed legislation requiring this education. Schools and other agencies, however, can initiate programs on a more informal basis.

In their training, teachers need to be made aware of their state's definition of maltreatment and the procedure of the child protection agency (CPA) in responding to reports. Additional information should include how, what, and when to report all kinds of abuse and neglect and ways to obtain feedback from the CPA about the accuracy of their reporting. Other objectives in the training program should include methods of keeping complete records of the child's disclosure and ways in which the coordination and collaboration between schools, the CPA, and law enforcement agencies can be improved. In addition, all teachers should be reassured about the nonpunitive objectives of the CPA, which are the following: to stop the child maltreatment, to ensure protection for the child, and to assist the families with necessary services (Besharov, 1990).

REACTING AND COMMUNICATING
WITH A CHILD WHO HAS BEEN MALTREATED

If a child confides in a teacher that he or she has been maltreated, there are a number of general recommendations and specific guidelines for reacting to the child's disclosure and communicating further, if necessary, to confirm the suspicion of the abuse or neglect (Sattler, 1998):

1. Sufficient time should be allocated for the interview, but the interview should be discontinued when the child appears tired or wants to stop.
2. The teacher should listen carefully to everything said by the child and follow up on any leads about the maltreatment.
3. The teacher should try to listen without bias or previous expectations.
4. Prompts should be avoided. For example, the teacher should not ask, "Did your uncle do it?" when the child never mentioned the uncle.
5. Uncomplicated syntax should be used when asking questions. For example, the teacher can ask, "What happened?" rather than say, "Search your memory and relate what occurred."
6. The teacher must avoid questions that imply the child is to blame, such as, "Why did you make her angry?"
7. The teacher should accept what the child is saying and be supportive because the child may be afraid and feel guilty about disclosing family secrets. The act of disclosure is often traumatic for the child.

Turnbull, Turnbull, Shank, and Leal (1999) provided a number of specific guidelines for a teacher to follow when a student discloses abuse or neglect. First, the teacher should avoid promising the child that the information will be kept confidential because teachers are mandated to report suspected maltreatment. The teacher can, however, promise to inform the student about any person contacted and the reasons for the communication. Second, the teacher should be nonjudgmental and encourage the child to talk freely. It is important for the teacher to watch the child for cues about how he or she wants the teacher to physically respond. Some children want to be hugged; others prefer not to be touched. Third, it is important for the teacher to reassure the student that he or she did what was right by telling about the maltreatment. The teacher should not allow the child to feel that his or her behavior caused the maltreatment or troubles in the family. Fourth, the teacher should not make derogatory comments about the alleged offenders. The child may still care about the abuser and may retract his or her statement so that the abuser will not get into trouble. Fifth, the teacher must take what the student says very seriously. According to some studies, children who are maltreated who are listened to with empathy, caring, and seriousness are better able to cope with their situations (Turnbull et al., 1999). Finally, the teacher should reassure the child that he or she will be there to help and will take action to stop the maltreatment.

Tower (1992) also has made some helpful suggestions for teachers when children confide their maltreatment. These are divided into two categories: what to do and what not to do. The following is a modified summary of what a teacher should do when a child confides in him or her:

1. The student should be reassured that the teacher trusts him or her.
2. Privacy should be provided for the child when he or she is confiding in the teacher. A place such as an empty classroom may be used.
3. The teacher should sit beside, not across from, the student.
4. Language should be used that is developmentally appropriate and easily understood.
5. If the teacher does not understand what the child is saying, he or she should ask for clarification.
6. The student should be reassured that if a question has to be repeated, it is not because he or she gave wrong answers.
7. It is important for the teacher to inform the child of any actions he or she is planning to take related to the interviews.

The following is a modified summary of what a teacher should not do when a child confides in him or her (Tower, 1992):

1. The teacher should not criticize or make fun of the language used by the student when he or she talks about his or her maltreatment.
2. The teacher should not ask leading questions that suggest answers.

3. If the child appears uncomfortable or reluctant to talk, the teacher should not probe further.
4. The teacher should not coerce or threaten the child to obtain more information.
5. During the talk, there should not be multiple questioners because they may intimidate the child and make him or her afraid to talk.
6. The teacher should not pressure the student to remove any clothing to show him or her evidence of the physical or sexual abuse.

To increase the accuracy of the communication and to be emotionally supportive, Kemp (1998) reminded teachers to give the child permission not to answer questions that are too difficult. Open-ended questions are better for obtaining information than questions that can be answered with a "yes" or a "no." Another way of obtaining more accurate information is for the teacher to encourage the child to make corrections if he or she has misinterpreted the child's story of abuse or neglect. The teacher is also reminded to keep careful records and document what was said when the child disclosed information about the maltreatment. If necessary, this documentation can assist the child protection and law enforcement agencies in their investigations. The final important reminder for the teacher is to remember that when communicating with a child who is disclosing maltreatment, the teacher plays three roles. The first role is that of being a mandated reporter; the second role is to protect the child; and the third role is to be a helper, if possible, to the troubled families. All three of these roles are ethically and morally based, but the first one, that of being a mandated reporter, is a legal responsibility.

COMMUNICATING WITH THE FAMILY

If it is necessary to communicate with family members about the suspected child maltreatment, Tower (1992) offered some helpful advice for teachers: The family should be aware of the teacher's legal obligations to report suspected abuse or neglect. This information needs to be stated in the school's policies so that the parents can give their informed consent when their child begins school. Then, if a teacher needs to report suspected abuse, the parents can be reminded that they have previously consented to this legal action and that the school personnel will be as supportive as possible. This reassurance can lessen the possible hostility of the family members toward the teacher.

If the family members want to discuss the report with the teacher, the meeting should be private and take place in a non-threatening atmosphere, such as in an empty classroom. The child should not be present, as he or she may be under extreme pressure to retract his or her statement when confronted with angry family members. The teacher should answer any questions about the reasons for the report in a direct and professional manner. The teacher should not attempt to prove that the maltreatment happened. This is the duty of the child protective and law enforcement personnel. It also is not the role of the teacher to pry into irrelevant family matters or to place blame or make judgments about the alleged abusers. As previously stated, teachers only have to be suspicious about the maltreatment to make a report.

Behaviors and Explanations
from Family Members that Can Cause Suspicion

According to Nunnelly and Fields (1999) and Sattler (1998), the following is a checklist of questions about a child's caregiver that teachers can ask themselves to confirm or refute their suspicions of child maltreatment:

1. In the case of physical abuse, does the explanation of the caregiver conflict with the appearance of the injury on the child?
2. If there are two or more caregivers, do they offer different explanations of the maltreatment?
3. Does the caregiver give a reason for the suspicious event that is not consistent with the child's developmental level? For example, a caregiver explains that the 2-month-old infant crawled to the hot stove and burned him- or herself.
4. Does the caregiver's description of the reasons for the injury not match with the child's disclosure?
5. Does the caregiver keep changing his or her story when giving reasons for the suspected abuse?
6. Does the caregiver make multiple excuses for the child's maltreatment or try to minimize it? For example, does the caregiver say that there is nothing wrong with physical punishment because it makes the child behave?
7. Does the caregiver constantly belittle the child and criticize his or her behaviors?
8. Does the caregiver not show concern for the children's injuries?

9. Does the caregiver have unrealistic and developmentally inappropriate expectations of the child?
10. Does the caregiver blame the child's siblings for the abuse when they are developmentally incapable of it? For example, does the caregiver blame the child's 2-year-old brother for repeatedly shaking and slamming the child against the wall?

Although a teacher's suspicions may be increased by certain responses given by caregivers, a positive attitude toward these individuals is best. The teacher can view the meetings with these family members as initial steps in helping them to stop the child maltreatment if later the CPA confirms that indeed the child has been maltreated.

ETHICAL CONCERNS ABOUT FAMILY PRIVACY

Laws against child maltreatment imply that in cases of suspected abuse or neglect, the rights of the children to protection supersedes the rights of the families to privacy and noninterference in their lives (Child Abuse Prevention and Treatment Act of 1974 [PL 93-247]; Kemp, 1998). In typical criminal cases, Americans value the presumption in the laws that a person is innocent until proven guilty and has the right to self-defense (Besharov, 1990). Because of the sympathy, anger, and concern aroused by suspected child maltreatment, however, some mandated reporters assume the alleged perpetrator's guilt ahead of time. This is in conflict with U.S. laws, and parental rights need to be respected for the sake of the family and the children.

Reports of suspected abuse can be offensive, intrusive, and humiliating to innocent family members. Even if the allegations are inaccurate, the family can still feel stigmatized by the investigation. Therefore, teachers must remember that only their suspicions are being reported and assume the family members are innocent until proven otherwise. Teachers might try to imagine their own anxiety and apprehension if they were accused of maltreatment without the protection of due process. Whenever possible, it is recommended that follow-up visits be made by the teachers to share the results of the investigations. If the maltreatment is disproven, the family members should have the opportunity to share their feelings and be reassured of the school's support (Besharov, 1994).

It is possible to protect the rights of parents without forgetting about the responsibilities of the mandated reporters to report suspected maltreatment and the right of children to protection. Every effort should be made by teachers to avoid bias and prejudice and to be objective in their reporting. The primary reasons for reporting their suspicions are to stop any maltreatment, to provide safety for the child, and to refer the troubled family members for needed services and rehabilitation.

POSSIBLE PSYCHOLOGICAL
CONSEQUENCES OF REPORTING FOR TEACHERS

Teachers may experience both positive and negative psychological consequences when they report suspected maltreatment. On one hand, if the report is substantiated, they can feel relief that their students are protected from further maltreatment and satisfaction that they have done what was right. On the other hand, there can be upsetting emotional consequences. Teachers are often the first people to whom children turn in times of crisis because of their trust in them and because of the teachers' availability. When initially learning about abuse, feelings of anger and hostility toward the alleged perpetrators and of concern and sympathy for the children are common. These feelings may arouse unpleasant memories if these professionals also were victims of maltreatment in their childhood.

The actual process of reporting can be frustrating for teachers if they are not knowledgeable about the laws and definitions of maltreatment. Misperceptions about the role of the teacher in the reporting process are common. For example, many teachers believe that they have to prove the abuse, that the family must be informed before making their reports, or that they are personally liable when they report in good faith. Other misunderstandings can arise from the cultural diversity of families and professionals, such as variance in their definitions of abuse, appropriate discipline, parenting techniques, and views of corporal punishment. Additional concerns include the teachers' fears that their rapport with families is threatened, that they may have to testify against them in court, that they will be harassed by angry offenders, or that reporting is a betrayal of the family.

Support for Teachers

Reporting suspected child abuse can be traumatic. Teachers may ask themselves the following questions: Will the families break up? Will the children be taken away and blame me for their removal from their homes? Will the alleged offenders threaten me? Will the children be safe, or will there be more maltreatment? Emotional support can be essential at this time in order for the teachers to relieve any guilt or uncertainty that they were correct in reporting their suspicions.

Nunnelley and Fields (1999) provided some recommendations about how to obtain this support. The first recommendation is to realize that these feelings are not uncommon and can be expected. The next suggestion is to join or form a support group of other educators who have been in this situation. These support groups may provide both empathy and reassurance that the teachers have done what was legally, ethically, and morally right. The third recommendation is to talk to supportive school counselors, psychologists, social workers, and administrators about their feelings. The fourth suggestion is to participate in professional meetings that discuss the effects that reporting has on teachers. The last recommendation is to contact relevant organizations for assistance, such as the Childhelp USA National Child Abuse Hotline ([800] 4-A-CHILD; http://www.childhelpusa. org/child/hotline.htm) or Prevent Child Abuse America (200 S. Michigan Avenue, Chicago, IL 60604-2404; [312] 663-3520; http://www. childabuse.org). As previously mentioned, even though teachers may have disturbing feelings about reporting, it is their legal mandate to report their suspicions of child maltreatment. A child's right to protection is paramount.

POSSIBLE PSYCHOLOGICAL
CONSEQUENCES OF DISCLOSURE FOR CHILDREN

In addition to teachers, children who are maltreated may experience positive or negative emotional consequences when they disclose their maltreatment. The positive emotions are relief from anxiety and feelings of safety and protection from further abuse. Possible negative feelings are worries about whether they have acted in the right manner by disclosing the maltreatment. A child may ask him- or herself the following questions: Will I be responsible for the break-up of my family? Will I be sent away? Will my teachers believe my explanation of the maltreatment? Will my family accuse me of lying? Will I be safe and protected from more abuse by the alleged offender(s)? Will I get innocent family members in trouble? Will they still love and care for me?

These negative feelings make emotional support essential for children who have been maltreated. Teachers can provide the needed emotional support to these children by doing the following. The teacher needs to listen to the child's statements without making judgments. The teacher can be emotionally available to validate the child's feelings by saying, "You seem to be scared. Has something made you afraid?" The teacher can watch the child for cues on how to physically respond to the disclosures. As stated previously, some children may want to be hugged, whereas others prefer not be touched. The teacher should reassure the child who disclosed the maltreatment by telling them they made the right decision to confide about the abuse. The child should not be blamed or made to feel responsible for the abuse. The abuser is the one who is responsible. The teacher can further reduce the student's anxiety by informing him or her of every step in the reporting process. In addition, the teacher can be a positive role model of nonviolent problem solving and positive coping skills for the child who lacks this modeling by his or her caregivers at home (Lambie, 2000). The teacher also can assist the child in devising a safety plan in which he or she can notify trusted adults about further maltreatment and escape from the offender.

POSSIBLE PSYCHOLOGICAL
CONSEQUENCES FOR FAMILY MEMBERS

Both positive and negative feelings can be aroused in family members when they discover the child's disclosure. If they are innocent and did not know about the abuse, feelings of shock and concern for the child and hostility toward the alleged perpetrator are common. If they have contributed to or know about the maltreatment, they may deny any knowledge of it and accuse the youngster of causing troubles in the family. They may fear that the family will break up as a result of the child's story; that they will lose custody of him or her; or, if the alleged offender is the breadwinner in the family, that he or she will be imprisoned and not be able to support the other family members. They may also have hostility toward the teacher. The teacher can remind the family members that he or she is reporting the suspicions because of his or her legal responsibilities and that he or she is not proving the maltreatment.

It is important for the teacher to continue to have positive communication with the family members, to refer them for services that reduce stress by meeting their needs, and to encourage school involvement by participating in conferences and meetings. Emphasizing their strengths and achievements can increase the pride of the family members in the child. If the caregivers or parents have unrealistic expectations of the child, they can be referred to parenting programs that emphasize knowledge of child development, positive parenting practices, and developmentally appropriate objectives for children. Another recommendation is for the teacher to work from a family strength model rather than from a deficit model. This can be accomplished by identifying strengths and achievements of family members that can be used to combat maltreatment and improve their caregiving practices (Reppucci et al., 1997).

POSSIBLE PSYCHOLOGICAL CONSEQUENCES FOR THE ALLEGED OFFENDERS

If the alleged offender is actually guilty, he or she often will deny any knowledge about the abusive incident, distort the child's information, or state that he or she does not remember any details of the maltreatment. In many instances, the abuser is afraid that he or she will be caught and display his or her fears by being extremely angry with the child for disclosing the maltreatment. It is also very common for an alleged offender to be hostile toward the teacher. The offender may blame the child's behavior as the cause for the maltreatment by saying, "She made me do it." Other rationalizations consist of minimizing the severity of the abuse, bargaining with the teacher not to report a "little" incident, or pleading that the maltreatment was beyond his or her control and should not be reported because of his or her overwhelming financial or emotional problems (Furniss, 1991). When questioning the family members of the child who has disclosed maltreatment, whether they are found later to be innocent or guilty, the teacher needs to take a nonjudgmental approach and remind the family members again that the reports are about the suspicions of maltreatment and not about proof of it. There may be concerns for the teacher's safety if the alleged abuser threatens him or her, so it is always important to have supportive personnel nearby and to terminate the meeting if there are any safety concerns. Accusations of guilt and blame should be avoided during the meeting. If the alleged abusers are found to be innocent, the teacher should meet with them to give them the chance to express any residual feelings and to reassure them that the school personnel know about their innocence.

IMPORTANCE OF THE FEEDBACK FROM THE REPORT

After teachers make a report, it is important for them to receive feedback on the results of the investigations of child maltreatment. Reporters want to know if their suspicions were or were not confirmed. This feedback improves the quality and accuracy of their reporting. If the teachers are not informed about the results of the

CPA investigation, they may believe that reporting is ineffectual and be reluctant to make future reports even when they are legally mandated to do so. In addition, the communication with the CPA will allow them to correct any misinterpretations of their statements. Another benefit of the feedback from the report is that the teachers will continue to monitor for further abuse and better ensure the safety of their students.

Teachers often are not given this feedback from the CPA. The following are several reasons for this lack of information: 1) CPA personnel are overloaded with cases and do not take the time to tell reporters the results of the investigations, 2) CPA personnel do not realize the importance of feedback for the teachers, and 3) CPA personnel believe that the information is confidential and cannot be released to the reporters. According to Besharov (1990), this last concern is false, as there are no legal reasons for not revealing the information. The teachers deserve the explanations and should be advised about the accuracy of their reports. The extent of information given to the teachers, however, must be balanced with the privacy rights of the family. The teachers should be told, at the very least, about the results of the investigations and whether their suspicions were correct. This will enable the teachers to better assist children who have been maltreated and their troubled families.

CONCLUSION

As previously stated, the role of teachers as mandated reporters is multifaceted because they are not only legally required to report maltreatment, but they are ethically and morally responsible, as much as possible, for its prevention and for protection of their students. They also have a role to play in assisting the families by referring them to needed services so that the maltreatment is stopped. Chapter 5 examines the significant role of teachers as advocates for inclusive services for children who are maltreated and their families; the training necessary for this role; the importance of teamwork and collaboration with families, other professionals, community members, and relevant organizations; and the ways teachers can influence public policies so that more resources will be provided to meet these challenges.

5

TEACHERS AS ADVOCATES

"If one child feels threatened, alone, or disconnected, then all children are not safe" (Litow, 1996, p. 1). This sentiment, expressed by Dr. Litow, an educator, points to the necessity for all teachers to advocate for all of the children who are maltreated and academically at risk and their families. This chapter first examines the meaning of advocacy. Then, the preparation needed for the role of advocate, desired competencies, and teachers' ethical responsibilities are discussed. Next, the issues that require teachers' advocacy in the prevention and intervention for child maltreatment are described. These include advocacy for early intervention, full service or integrated service schools (schools that offer a variety of services, including child care, health care, counseling, and so forth), collaboration and teamwork, necessary teacher training, positive changes in public policy, future research concerning prevention and intervention, and support for the rights of children who are at risk.

THE MEANING OF ADVOCACY

Advocacy is defined by Fennimore as "a personal commitment to active involvement in the lives of children" (1989, p. 4). The goal of this commitment when applied to children who are at risk is to remove the risk so that they can develop their abilities to the optimum and become productive, caring adults. Advocacy for them requires an emotional investment in empathy, a recognition of their needs, and a desire to help them meet these needs (Berger, 2000). As advocates, teachers not only must accept responsibility for these students' academic progress but for their socioemotional development as well. There are a number of reasons for accepting these responsibilities: Legally, teachers are mandated to report suspected child maltreatment; morally and ethically, teachers are concerned about their students' grief and pain from the abuse and neglect; and professionally, teachers are required to combat the maltreatment (MacIntyre, 1990). All teachers have a stake in the well-being of children who are at risk because this involvement is essential for the economic, social, educational, and cultural survival of the American society. If teachers do not try to prevent child maltreatment, social ills often increase (e.g., more crime, delinquency, teenage parenting, school dropouts, mental illness, substance abuse, poverty, and chronic unemployment) (Walker & Sprague, 1999; Westman, 1996).

PREPARATION FOR THE ROLE OF THE ADVOCATE

Berger (2000) and Fiedler (2000) provided suggestions about how teachers can first prepare themselves for the advocate role. The following is a modified summary applied to children who are maltreated and at risk for academic failure:

1. Teachers need to regard children as being a protected class of citizens. This has a special meaning when teaching children who are maltreated who may desperately need protection and both physical and psychological safety.
2. Teachers should recognize the signs and symptoms of child abuse and neglect and be informed about the rights of children not to be maltreated.
3. Teachers need to understand how social changes have evolved in American society. This information will assist them in advocating for changes in public policy that will benefit children at risk and their families.
4. Teachers should be aware of the effects of adverse social and economic conditions, which may result in child maltreatment.
5. School personnel should be able to identify and contact community resources that can assist families in stopping their child maltreatment.

The next step in preparation to be child advocates is to be knowledgeable about the goals developed by the National Education Goals Panel (1994). Originally, the goals were to be fulfilled by the year 2000; however, the year 2000 has passed, and these goals have not yet been achieved. The goals are still appropriate, however, and can be related to teachers' objectives for children who are at risk. Teachers' increasing awareness of the issues concerning child maltreatment can be an important step toward achieving these goals. The following is an adapted summary of the goals developed by the National Education Goals Panel (1994):

- *Goal 1: All American children will be ready to learn.* This is a special challenge when teaching children who are abused or neglected who may not be ready to learn because of the detrimental effects on their early development from the maltreatment.
- *Goal 2: The number of high school graduates will increase at least to 90%.* This objective has a special meaning when applied to students who are at risk who may lack the motivation to remain in school.
- *Goal 3: American students will leave Grades 4, 8, and 12 having demonstrated competency in challenging subject matter, including English, mathematics, science, history, and geography; and every school in America will ensure that all students learn to use their minds well so that they may be prepared for responsible citizenship, further learning, and productive employment in America's modern economy.* This goal represents a great challenge to teachers of children who are maltreated because the research indicates that these students have particular difficulty with language, mathematics, and abstract thinking (Barnett, 1997; Eckenrode, Laird, & Doris, 1993; Vondra, Barnett, & Cicchetti, 1990).
- *Goal 4: The U.S. teaching force will have access to services for the continual improvement of their professional skills and the opportunity to acquire the knowledge and skills needed to instruct and prepare all American students for the next century.* This goal, when applied to teaching students who are at risk, stresses the necessity for teachers to keep abreast of new methods of teaching that can assist these children in being successful in school.
- *Goal 5: U.S. students will be the first in the world in science and math achievement.* Again, when applying this goal to students who are at risk, teachers are challenged to learn new methods of instruction that are effective for these students who may have special difficulties with these subjects (Barnett, 1997; Lowenthal, 1996).
- *Goal 6: Every American adult will be literate and will possess the necessary knowledge and skills to compete in a global economy and exercise the rights and responsibilities of citizenship.* To meet this challenge, as it relates to children who are at risk, teachers should do everything within their power to prevent child maltreatment so that their students feel secure, feel safe,

and are motivated to learn and to become literate, productive adults.

- *Goal 7: Every school in America will be free of drugs and violence and will offer a disciplined environment conducive to learning.* In applying this goal to students who are at risk, teachers need to model and teach nonviolent behavior, conflict management, and constructive problem-solving skills so that the students learn these behaviors, which may not be modeled in their homes.
- *Goal 8: Every school will promote partnerships that will increase parental involvement and participation in promoting the social-emotional and academic growth of children.* The goal of increasing parental involvement is another special challenge when teachers work with families that may appear resistant, uninvolved, or difficult to reach.

Fulfilling these goals will require much effort, training, dedication, and caring for teachers of students who are at risk. It is the teachers' responsibility as teacher advocates, however, to prepare themselves to meet these challenges.

Additional Steps in Preparation to Be Advocates

Another step teachers can take in preparation for their role as advocates is to understand clearly the reasons why teachers are fitted for this role (Fiedler, 2000). All children need adults to represent and support them. Because teachers are with students daily, they have opportunities to do this for students who are at risk. Because of their professional training, teachers can have significant insight about the needs of each child who is maltreated. Also, as professionals, teachers may be able to circumvent some bureaucratic red tape to obtain essential services for children who are at risk and their families. They can keep track of not only the cognitive performance but also of the social-emotional development of their students. Teachers have opportunities to involve other community members in their advocacy efforts, including families who may be at risk.

COMPETENCIES FOR THE ROLE OF ADVOCATE

Fiedler (2000), Thorp and McCollum (1994), and Weissbourd (1996) described the desired competencies for the advocate role. Fiedler (2000) divided these competencies into three areas: dispositions, knowledge, and skills. The area of dispositions concerns the values that professionals have regarding advocacy. Effective advocates believe that support for students who are at risk and their families is part of their job responsibilities. Teachers who are advocates are committed to the values of empathy and caring when they work with these students and their families. They display these values when they assist the children and families in obtaining access to necessary resources to meet their needs (Thorp & McCollum, 1994). Teachers who have a disposition toward advocacy are motivated to help the caregivers to stop child maltreatment. In addition, they are willing to acquire the necessary skills to accomplish these goals (Weissbourd, 1996).

The second area of competency relates to the knowledge that teachers need for effective advocacy. Teachers should be informed about relevant legislation concerning child maltreatment, including changes they would like to see that would benefit the children. In addition, knowledge of conflict management and constructive problem-solving techniques is essential for solving disputes that may arise during the process of advocacy.

The last area of competency consists of personal skills needed by teachers. These are skills in communication with others to gain their support for students who are at risk; skills in teamwork with other school personnel, professionals, and community members to improve services for children who are maltreated and their families; and skills and faith in their personal efficacy or in the belief that advocacy can make a positive difference for the students who are at risk and their families (Fiedler, 2000; Weissbourd, 1996).

ETHICAL RESPONSIBILITIES

Together with appropriate competencies, awareness of one's ethical responsibilities is important for teachers. According to Goens (1996) and Strike, Haller, and Soltis (1998), the teachers' code of ethics determines which behaviors they consider right and which ones they consider wrong. Ethics then serves as a guide to what actions are morally good (Heron, Martz, & Margolis, 1996; Nelson, 1994).

There are some principles that pertain to teachers' ethical responsibilities and moral behaviors when they advocate for children who are at risk. These are provided in the ethical code developed by the National Association for the Education of Young Children (NAEYC; 1998). An adapted summary is that teachers need to appreciate the special vulnerability of children in their care. Most important, teachers should do no harm to them or participate in any action that exploits, degrades, emotionally abuses, or physically harms them.

The next principle is to involve all those who possess relevant information (including family members, school personnel, other professionals, and community members) in decision-making that may assist students who are at risk. The third principle concerns modifications that teachers should be willing to make in teaching strategies, curricula, and school environments when necessary for a child who is at risk to gain maximum benefit from the school program. If the teachers' efforts are not successful so that the child benefits from them, then they have the responsibility to communicate with the family and relevant specialists in order to identify a more successful environment for the child. Teachers also need to help the family in arranging for the new placement. The next principle is that it is important for teachers to be informed about the symptoms of child maltreatment so that they can report their reasonable suspicions to the child protection agency (CPA) to investigate. If a teacher does report his or her reasonable suspicion, then he or she needs to follow-up in regard to what action was taken if the child needed protection. If protection is not provided, then the teacher and the agency personnel have mutual responsibilities to improve the services. The last ethical principle discussed is that when teachers are aware of a practice or environment that endangers their students, their duty is to inform others who can remedy this state of affairs and protect the children from similar situations. Carrying out these ethical responsibilities is an integral part of teachers' jobs (NAEYC, 1998).

Characteristics of Ethical Teachers

A number of personal qualities are characteristic of ethical teacher advocates. Teachers need to model and demonstrate them in their advocacy (Greenspan & Negron, 1994). These characteristics are candor, discretion, diligence, fairness, avoidance of dual relationships, fostering of autonomy, and respect (Fiedler, 2000). Candor is exhibited by teachers who tell the truth to other professionals, students, and family members. Discretion is shown when confidential information is not disclosed by teachers in their comments to uninvolved individuals. Diligence is displayed by teachers who are dedicated to their advocacy efforts. Fairness is demonstrated by teachers who have nondiscriminatory attitudes and regard toward others. Fairness also involves advocating for necessary services for all eligible students and their families regardless of their diverse cultural, linguistic, and socioeconomic backgrounds. Avoidance of dual relationships is displayed when teachers recognize that their primary responsibilities are toward their students. For example, if administrators refuse to report their teachers' reasonable suspicions of child maltreatment, then the teachers must report them even when their supervisors disapprove. Fostering of autonomy is exhibited when teachers work to enable family members who are at risk to independently have access to the services they need to prevent possible child abuse or neglect (Dunst, Trivette, & Deal, 1994). Respect is displayed when teachers treat their students who are at risk and their families with dignity and empathy. When teachers model these abilities, they demonstrate the characteristics of ethical teachers.

ISSUES THAT REQUIRE TEACHERS' ADVOCACY

The following issues can require the advocacy of teachers who work with students who are maltreated and are academically at risk and their families: early intervention, full service or integrated service schools, collaboration and teaming, effective teacher training, changes in public policies, future research, and support for the rights of children.

Advocacy for Early Intervention

When teachers advocate for early intervention and prevention of child maltreatment, they make a wise investment in America's future. It is in the public's interest to support early intervention, as the research indicates that it will increase the number of productive, caring citizens and reduce the number who require welfare, special education, mental and physical health services, child protective services, and correctional institutions (Gunnar, Broderson, Krueger, & Rigatuso, 1996; Newberger, 1997; Reyome, 1993). The costs in human suffering, loss of potential, and actual money from trying to heal or remediate children who are maltreated can be much more than the costs of prevention by promoting healthy development in all areas in early childhood (Ounce of Prevention Fund, 1996). It is essential that teachers recognize that when children are maltreated during their early years of life, the results can be lost abilities and inadequate learning throughout their entire lifetimes (Barnett, 1997).

Intervention efforts need to start as soon as possible when the maltreatment is confirmed (Cicchetti, Toth, & Hennessy, 1989; Zeanah & Scheeringa, 1996). With quick action by teachers, mental health specialists, social workers, and protective services, the chances of lessening the damage from abuse and neglect are increased. The earlier the intervention, the more resilience is enhanced and later development is facilitated. The importance of helping every child who is abused or neglected with an individualized intervention plan cannot be emphasized enough. Cook, Tessier, and Klein (2000) recommend that at preschool, children who are maltreated be provided with the most nurturing, predictable, and responsive environments possible so that they will increase their self-confidence, feel protected, and gain a sense of mastery and competence.

The major providers of early childhood experiences usually are the parents. If they are at risk for child maltreatment, it is important to facilitate their involvement in prevention, treatment, and intervention programs. Teachers need to advocate for more parent education classes that discuss typical child development so that parental expectations are developmentally appropriate for their children. The more that caregivers who are at risk can improve their interactions with the children, the more likely maltreatment will be prevented (Newberger, 1997). If necessary, caregivers who are at risk should be provided with therapeutic services to enable them to establish more supportive home environments (Cicchetti et al., 1989; Dunst et al., 1994). Thus, advocacy for early prevention and intervention is critically important for teachers when assisting children who are maltreated and their families.

Advocacy for Services

As previously mentioned, a range of community services may be necessary for families at risk of child abuse and neglect. To better assist the children and their family members, positive relationships need to be built between the schools and community-based social service agencies. One way that it can be made easier for families to have access to the services of these agencies is to provide them at convenient school sites. The schools that offer them have been referred to as integrated service schools (Hurd, Lerner, & Alten, 1999). Teacher advocates should support integrated service schools because they offer a coordinated approach in providing necessary resources to students who are at risk and their families. These schools focus on the prevention of problems; academic readiness and success; and the alleviation of stressors, such as isolation, poverty, ill health, and unemployment (Larson, Gumby, Shiono, Lewit, & Behrman, 1992). They offer "one-stop" shopping for family members who need these services (Dryfoos, 1994). Generally, a variety of services are offered, which include child care, health services, counseling, job placement, gang diversion programs, special programs for dropouts, sports activities, literacy development, parenting classes, and English as a second language programs. These services cut across traditional social, health, and educational systems (Lowenthal, 1996).

The traditional system of established child services is often fragmented and confusing for families to gain access to, and school personnel alone are often ill-equipped to handle the families' problems. Because schools are enduring institutions in the communities, however, they typically have the most long-term contacts with students and their families. Thus, they have the potential to become the hub of a system of services and to serve as a link between the system and the families. In economic terms, as previously discussed, prevention appears more cost effective than later solutions to problems with child abuse and neglect. As another example, there seems to be a correlation between dropping out of school and committing a crime (Hodgkinson, 1989). Drop-out prevention is cheaper in the long run than the cost of crime, including that of building new prisons.

Teachers also should advocate integrated service schools because they can target a variety of children who are at risk and their families, not only those who have been maltreated (e.g., children of migrant workers, children who are homeless, children with disabilities, children with chronic conditions). Some of these children may have poor school attendance and performance records (Olenick & McCroskey, 1992). To assist these students, connections need to be made between the schools and social services in the community, which are easier to achieve in integrated service schools. Some states (e.g., California, Florida, Illinois, Mississippi, New Jersey) already have begun to implement models that expand the social and health services offered at local schools along with their customary educational curricula (Lowenthal, 1996).

Although there appears to be no one best model of an inclusive service school, teachers can advocate for their local schools to include the following criteria for successful programs (Robinson, 1990): The programs should be family focused, designed to meet community needs, and oriented toward the prevention of problems such as child maltreatment. Schools with integrated services should be more open to people in the local community, including students, families, community members, school personnel, and related services professionals. School-based personnel should include not only traditional educational professionals but also community residents and service providers. Some schools in high-risk areas may be known as human development sites rather than just academic environments (Bucci & Reitzhammer, 1992). The primary responsibility of the teachers in an inclusive school is to educate their students, but they will also know how to refer the children and their families to the necessary services at the school sites.

School administrators can play a key part in this teacher role expansion by their continued support and encouragement. Careful planning is needed on the part of the school staff, service agencies, community leaders, families, and students in order to decide on the essential services needed in the local communities. In addition, school personnel may have to enhance their skills in collaborative leaderships and decision making with community agencies.

Teachers need to advocate for better training to work in integrated service schools. Curricula for students in preservice training and workshops for in-service teachers should include more information about the roles of related services providers. A number of preservice and in-service teachers need to learn skills of collaboration and teamwork with other helping professionals and community representatives (Bailey, 1996). Positive attitudes should be fostered about the values of integrated service schools. Field experiences and practica for teachers and service providers need to be expanded to include more school-based full-service sites in which teachers can learn first-hand how to cooperate with one another.

Advocacy also is called for to obtain additional federal funding and support to assist the efforts of state and local governments to establish more integrated service schools. Federal leadership is required to change funding and eligibility restrictions in order to make maximum use of funds from programs such as Medicaid to provide inclusive services. Several national movements have supported these services at schools. For example, a legislative initiative called the Family Support Act (FSA) of 1988, PL 100-48, was designed to strengthen families as part of the welfare system. It supports the coordination of services by recognizing the cooperative efforts of education, vocational training, social services, and health agencies as central to helping children and families on welfare. The FSA encourages a close relationship among social, health, and educational programs to assist these families. Another successful example is Project Head Start (Buscemi, Bennett, Thomas, & Deluca, 1995), which was created as a national full-service preschool program for children and their families from low socioeconomic backgrounds. In conclusion, teacher advocacy is important to obtain these full service programs at school sites that support and provide for the needs of children who are at risk and their family members.

THE NECESSITY FOR COLLABORATION AND TEAMING

Integrated service schools require skills in collaboration and team-work among personnel, a variety of professionals, families, and other community members. The following section defines collaboration, describes its important principles, and discusses types of teams and teamwork.

The Meaning and Principles of Collaboration

Collaboration has been defined by Friend and Cook as "a style for direct interaction between at least two coequal parties voluntarily engaged in decision making as they work toward a common goal" (1992, p. 5). A related definition is provided by Graden and Bauer who defined collaboration as "a fundamental way of working to-gether in a true partnership" (1992, p. 88). Principles of effective col-laboration are the following (Vandercook, York, & Sullivan, 1993):

1. When establishing mutual goals, successful collaborators de-velop a positive relationship with each other and agree on a com-mon philosophy.
2. Participation is voluntary, which means that no one is forced to collaborate.
3. All collaborators have mutual and equal responsibilities to de-rive solutions to problems. In following this principle, teachers, other professionals, families, students, and interested com-munity members are encouraged to cooperate to fulfill the common goals of preventing and intervening against child mal-treatment. All participants also are responsible for the out-comes of the collaborative process. If success is achieved, then everyone can celebrate. If failure occurs, it is looked upon as a way of learning from errors.
4. Collaborators should share resources, which means that they must identify mutual resources and find ways of jointly sharing them.

All of these principles of effective collaboration stress the benefits of cooperation and the nonduplication of resources and services.

For successful collaboration, teachers with other participants need time to plan, communicate, problem-solve, and evaluate whether their solutions were successful. Collaborative skills for teachers include empathy; a positive, enthusiastic attitude; respect for all individuals involved in the collaboration; the ability to com-municate effectively and establish rapport; the ability to manage conflict; and the desire and ability to problem-solve and derive solutions cooperatively. Collaboration also requires knowledge of how to work on teams.

Types of Teams and Teamwork

There are actually three types of teams when working with families (Lerner, Lowenthal, & Egan, 1998): multidisciplinary, interdisciplinary, and transdisciplinary. On multidisciplinary teams, the professionals provide isolated services to families without consultation with other team members. This can lead to fragmented, duplicated services with confusing recommendations on how best to solve the problems of children who are at risk and their families. On this type of team, teachers and other participants work alone for the most part and do not obtain benefits from collaboration. In addition, input from family members is not considered important. On interdisciplinary teams, although each team member intervenes separately for the child and the family, the teammates do meet sometimes to discuss their recommendations. Families are considered members of the team, but their input into ways to solve their problems is regarded as secondary to that of professionals. On transdisciplinary teams, there is a sharing of roles between teachers, professionals, families, and community personnel. On these teams, there is an understanding between participants that each team member's goals cannot be achieved unless all of the teammates' goals are met. Every participant, including the family members, are encouraged to work together to find solutions to the problems of the children who are at risk and their families. This type of team is considered the most effective for integrated service schools because it avoids duplication of services, emphasizes cooperative teamwork, encourages the active and equal involvement of family members, and benefits the most from collaboration (Lerner, 2000).

ADVOCACY FOR EFFECTIVE TEACHER TRAINING

Training efforts should be improved and expanded both for students in preservice training and in-service educators to increase their awareness of types and signs of childhood abuse and neglect, legal regulations for reporting, referral procedures, ways to involve families that are at risk in partnerships, and better methods of teacher prevention and intervention. Advocacy is necessary for more coursework and in-service workshops that examine and discuss these issues. In this training, it is also important to point out the benefits of collaboration and cooperative teamwork, which demonstrate teachers' interrelated responsibilities with other representatives on the teams.

Personal Responsibilities of Teachers

As previously discussed, each teacher has the personal responsibility to become more informed about the issues of child abuse and neglect and to keep up-to-date with current research. Obtaining this information can be accomplished by reading relevant journals (e.g., *Journal of Child Abuse, Journal of Child Abuse and Neglect*), consulting with other professionals, and joining organizations that work to prevent child maltreatment, such as the National Committee to Prevent Child Abuse. Appendix A lists pertinent books, journals, videotapes, and audiotapes. Appendix B lists relevant organizations that advocate for children who are at risk and/or maltreated and their family members. Volunteering in special programs is another way to learn about and assist the children. An example is the Court Appointed Special Advocate (CASA) Program (Leung, 1996) in which volunteers are trained in many states to represent and support children who are maltreated in court proceedings. Information about the CASA Program in a certain area can be obtained by contacting the local protection or law enforcement agencies. All of these activities can help teachers to better comprehend and stay informed about child maltreatment and methods of prevention and intervention.

ADVOCACY FOR CHANGES IN PUBLIC POLICY

Another issue of importance for teacher advocates is the way to bring about changes in public policy to be more supportive of efforts to combat child abuse and neglect. Public policy has the responsibility to provide for the basic needs and safety of all citizens, and this is especially significant for children who are maltreated who may have a myriad of unmet needs. Influencing public policy is often necessary to institute changes at the local, state, and federal levels. The following section examines the types of policies needed to support prevention and intervention for child maltreatment, the steps teachers can take for public policy advocacy, the issues of funding, and the policies needed to support further research (Turnbull, Buchele-Ash, & Mitchell, 1994).

Types of Policies to Support

There are two kinds of policies to be considered in teachers' support for children who are at risk and their families: 1) communal and 2) individual and family. The communal perspective is that it is in the best interest of the community to further the child-rearing

competence of family members and to foster the healthy development of their children. The communal belief is that if this perspective is supported, the child, family, and community will benefit.
This viewpoint informs the family that the community expects the
family caregivers not to maltreat their children. When caregivers do
it anyway after getting warned, then the community representatives will remove the children from their custody and terminate
their custodial rights (Turnbull et al., 1994).

In contrast, the individual viewpoint allows the family to tell
the community, "Look, these children belong to us. How we raise
our children is not your business. It's a private matter. You are in-
fringing upon our rights as individuals when you tell us how we
should raise our children." It is necessary to balance both perspectives in a public policy. Teachers need to support policy reforms
that increase necessary services to families that are at risk who can
have easy access to them. Family members can be encouraged to
use them voluntarily. If needed to stop child maltreatment, however, involuntary means can be used, such as permanent cessation
of the caregivers' rights to their children who are removed from the
homes (Turnbull et al., 1994).

Activities for Public Policy Advocacy

There are a number of activities in which teacher advocates can participate to influence legislation and public policy to be more supportive and offer more services to combat child maltreatment. The
first is for teachers to contact their U.S. senators or representatives
by letter, e-mail, fax, or telephone to inform them about their support. A letter, e-mail, or fax should be personal, not a form letter, because personal correspondence is more meaningful and influential
to members of Congress (Berger, 2000). At the state level, teachers
can get in touch with their state senators and representatives to let
them know the public policies they support. A good time to reach
and influence these officials is before elections or when a bill that
pertains to child abuse and neglect is coming up for passage in the
Congress. Teachers may need to remind the legislators that their
votes do count! Teachers also can become more familiar with the
needs of children who are at risk and their families by visiting local
shelters for the homeless, juvenile courts, and temporary child care
residential centers (Berger, 2000).

Funding Issues

The type of programs that can assist children who are at-risk and
their families clearly cost money. It often is difficult for policy mak-

ers to allocate enough funds for this purpose when they also are asked to meet a myriad of other needs of their constituents. To add to these difficulties, public officials are expected to be fiscally responsible and keep taxes as low as possible. To complicate matters further, the fiscal benefits from combating child maltreatment are not usually apparent right away. They are obtained over a long period of time, such as when the children who receive assistance grow up to be productive and responsible adult citizens. If these benefits can be documented using existing and future positive research results, however, it will be easier for legislators to vote for the necessary funding. In the documented research, the economic benefits of helping the children and family members are described, such as healthier children and adults, better school readiness and achievement, fewer dropouts from school, less juvenile delinquency, a decrease in teen parenting, better work skills and productivity, a decrease in drug addiction, and less necessity for building jails (Barnett, 1997; Vondra et al., 1990). This information can help policy makers to vote for the needed resources (Ammerman & Baladerian, 1993; Turnbull et al., 1994).

ADVOCACY FOR FUTURE RESEARCH

Advocacy and support also are required for future research to help teachers learn more effective methods of prevention and intervention for child maltreatment. It is important to keep in mind that the interaction of multiple risk factors can lead to abuse and neglect. There usually is no one factor responsible for it. Therefore, future research needs to be multidimensional and involve children, families, and their environments (Ammerman & Baladerian, 1993). Barnett (1997) and Turnbull et al. (1999) provided other recommendations for future studies. A modified summary is that the research should be long term so that the results can be studied to see if they have lasting effects. There is a need for more treatment comparison studies in which behavior-based programs that emphasize parenting skills are compared with ecologically based ones that stress providing families with tangible benefits, such as child care, job training, and housing (Barnett, 1997). Family systems–based programs that stress interpersonal factors and the role of family history in maltreatment also can be compared with the other treatments to see which types of programs are the most successful in prevention and intervention for child abuse and neglect. Daro (1993) suggested that additional studies are needed of programs that enroll families that are severely dysfunctional because they are the most difficult to help and their number is growing. Because there is a current interest in attachment theory, which emphasizes the importance of the parent–infant bonding process, as a basis for programs, the efficacy of the programs should be studied to see if families that are maltreating their children, when given appropriate assistance, can improve their quality of attachment and interactions with their children and stop their abuse and neglect (Barnett, 1997; van IJzendoorn et al., 1995).

Multicomponent research is also desired, which includes the following topics: the effectiveness of counseling and child management training for parents who are at risk, the benefits of training in conflict management and problem solving for caregivers who are maltreating their children, the effects of social supports, interventions that try to reduce parental substance abuse, training in communicative skills to prevent the use of violence to meet needs, the efficacy of job training and assistance in job searches to eventually improve low socioeconomic status, ways to reduce violence in schools and communities, the long-term effectiveness of parent education and child management training, and the efficacy of integrated service schools over the long-term.

ADVOCACY FOR THE RIGHTS OF CHILDREN

Who speaks up for the rights of children? Everyone should, but the U.S. Advisory Board on Abuse and Neglect (Department of Health and Human Services, 1993) and the United Nations (1989) have already done so. A modified summary of their statements with the additions of special references to children who are maltreated and/or who are at risk is that all children have the right to protection and safety from maltreatment no matter who their caregivers are. They have the right to grow up in a nurturing, affectionate, and understanding atmosphere. The U.S. government, as part of the United Nations, has the responsibility and duty to protect its young citizens from harm. These children have the right to be treated with respect and dignity. In addition, they have the right to be represented in any judicial proceeding that affects them.

The Charter for Illinois Children (Voices for Illinois Children, 1999) also includes important rights for all children, values, and principles that not only involve children who are at risk but their families and teachers as well. A brief, adapted summary follows:

• Childhood is a sacred time that should be nurtured and celebrated.
• Basic necessities for children are family, safety, education, health, economic security, arts, recreation, and culture.

- All children need to belong to loving families and caring communities.
- All children deserve to have safe homes, schools, and communities.
- Children can learn from their mistakes, and all adults need to give them opportunities to do this.
- Every child is unique.
- No adult should ever give up on any child.

The values and principles affecting families include the need to protect the dignity and value the diversity of all families. Families should be provided with the skills, knowledge, and resources needed to sustain loving homes. Families are responsible for guiding and nurturing the total development of their children, including the physical, emotional, mental, moral, and spiritual areas. The values and principles that teachers should follow are to foster the learning of children; to respect each child's potential, abilities, and differences; to develop partnerships with students, families, and community members; to encourage the use of schools before and after the school day; to advocate for safe, clean, excellent, and well-funded schools; and to teach their students to value and respect diversities in people. Truly, teachers have many challenges to meet as educators and as community members to uphold these values and principles!

CONCLUSION

This chapter has examined the role of advocacy for teachers of children who are maltreated. A number of issues that require advocacy in the prevention and intervention of child maltreatment have been described. Chapter 6 discusses methods of working with families that are at risk in order to prevent child maltreatment.

6

FAMILY RISK FACTORS

This chapter discusses the prevention of and interventions for child maltreatment by examining ways in which teachers can assist families that are at risk for child abuse and neglect. As a background for this information, current definitions of what constitutes a family are examined. In addition, relevant theories are reviewed, including Maslow's *hierarchy of human needs*; the *ecological theory*; and the *transactional and family systems theories*, which were briefly mentioned in Chapter 2. Implications for teacher interventions then are discussed. The importance of a constructive and nonpunitive attitude toward families that are at risk for child maltreatment is then emphasized. Next, the teacher's role in family empowerment and in assisting caregivers in gaining access to the necessary supports and services is examined. The last section of the chapter focuses on the needs for communicative skills and sensitivity to family diversities, including cultural-linguistic and age diversities exemplified by teenage parenting. A teacher's understanding and work with families that are at risk can be of significant assistance to the family including the children in his or her classes who are maltreated.

CURRENT DEFINITIONS OF FAMILIES AND THEIR STRUCTURES

For many years, American families were described as being nuclear in their structures. The traditional nuclear family consisted of a married mother and father and their children (Copeland & White, 1991). Since the 1980s, however, this definition has broadened to include any group of people who consider themselves a family. This can include members related by blood or marriage as well as those who are not related but feel as though they are families because of their dedication to each other and their commitment to share their lives (Hanson & Lynch, 1992).

Alternative types of families include step- and blended families, extended families and kinships, same-gender partners, and single-parent families. According to Lynch (1998), the significant part of the definition of a family is that there is a feeling of belonging together and the desire to care for each other. There has been an increase in the number of alternative families with a corresponding decrease of nuclear families in American society. It has become imperative that this diversity in structure is not only accepted but is appreciated and respected by teachers and other professionals.

THEORIES OF FAMILY DEVELOPMENT

As a background for understanding and assisting families that are at risk, the following theories are reviewed: Maslow's Hierarchy of Human Needs (Maslow, 1954), the *ecological theory* (Bronfenbrenner, 1979), and a more comprehensive analysis of the *transactional* (Sameroff, 1995) and *family system theories* (Dunst et al., 1994; Turnbull et al., 1999).

Maslow's Hierarchy of Human Needs

Maslow's hierarchy of human needs theory suggests that all humans have basic needs, which are arranged in a hierarchy (Maslow, 1954). The first level consists of physical necessities, such as food, clothing, and shelter. The second level is concerned with needs for safety and security. The third level emphasizes the needs for love, belonging, and being valued by others. The fourth level focuses on self-esteem, and the fifth level is the necessity for self-actualization or the attainment of one's highest potential and psychological wholeness as a person (Kemp, 1998; Sattler, 1998). Self-actualization requires the achievement of all prior levels in the hierarchy. Maslow's hierarchy of human needs theory, when applied to families that are at risk, indicates that if the parents' basic physical needs are not met, there will be no time, motivation, or energy to provide their children with the higher level needs of security, love, affection, belonging, self-esteem, and self-actualization. In addition, there is an increased risk for child maltreatment because of the caregivers' frustration and anger when their basic needs continually are not met.

Ecological Theory

The ecological theory emphasizes the linkage of the individual not only to the family but also to the community and the larger environment (Bronfenbrenner, 1979). There is a reciprocal influence between these environments. Bronfenbrenner (1979) described four ecological systems that interact and can be pictured as circles enclosed into one another by size. The circles are labeled microsystems, mesosystems, exosystems, and macrosystems. Figure 5.1 illustrates these four ecological systems. The innermost and smallest circle, the microsystem, contains the immediate environment of the individual, such as the family environment. The mesosystem contains a number of microsystems, such as child care and school environments. The microsystems are linked together and influence each other, such as when the school influences the parents and vice versa. When the microsystems support one another, they have a positive impact on the child's development. When the mesosystem

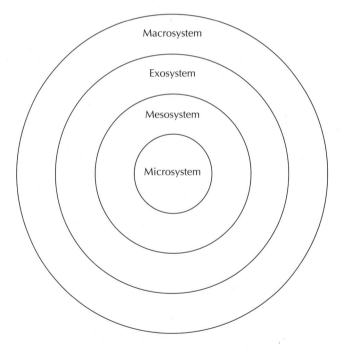

Figure 5.1. Four ecological systems. (*Sources:* Berger, 2000; Bronfenbrenner, 1979; & Hildebrand, Phenice, Gray, & Hines, 2000.)

is not directly involved with the children, it becomes what Bronfenbrenner (1979) termed the exosystem. The exosystem, however, can have an indirect effect on the lives of children. For example, the child welfare agency may not directly influence the children, but because it provides families with needed resources there are positive effects on child development. The macrosystem is the largest circle and is the farthest away from the children but still influences them. This system includes the cultural, political, social, religious, and economic values, practices, and actions of the larger environment. The implications for teachers is that in order to assist families that are at risk, they need to be aware of the prevailing beliefs, values, and practices of the larger socioeconomic, cultural, and political environments of the family members in addition to those of more immediate environments.

Transactional Theory

Proponents of the transactional theory view child development as a dynamic system of transactions between children, their caregivers, other family members, and their wider sociocultural environments (Sameroff, 1993, 1995). All of these transactions continually affect each other over time. For example, children will influence the actions of others by their behaviors, which are regulated by biological and genetic factors that include physical and mental health, temperaments, and rates of maturation. This theory then indicates that children are not just passive responders to events and interactions in their environments but actively shape their own lives. The combination of child characteristics and the effects of their environments have a tremendous impact on children's development. In addition, the transactional theory suggests that when caregivers are provided with needed resources, they can have more positive interactions with their children, which in turn will benefit their children's development. The implications for teachers are that they need to work with the students who are at risk and their families as well as with community agencies that can provide them with the necessary supports and services.

Family Systems Theory

The family systems theory was briefly referred to in Chapter 2. This section analyzes the theory's implications for teachers who work with families that are at risk and their children to prevent child maltreatment. The basic assumptions of the family systems theory are the following: 1) There is an interrelationship between all of the family members similar to any system whose parts relate to each other; 2) therefore, any change or intervention for one family member affects all members; 3) no person is isolated from the influences of the rest of the family members; and 4) the family is greater than the sum of its parts (Hanson & Lynch, 1992).

This theory hypothesizes that families are composed of subsystems, which are marital (parent–parent), parental (parent–child), sibling (child–child), and extrafamilial (additional individuals, such as extended family, friends, neighbors, and so forth). Interactions among these subsystems shape the behaviors of the family members. The ways that family members react in one subsystem, however, are not necessarily predictive of their behaviors in the other subsystems. For example, parents act differently in their interactions with each other than they do with their children. However, if there are stressors in one subsystem, such as domestic violence in the marital system, they will cause stress in the parental subsystem, which then adversely affects the relationship of the parent to the child. This is illustrated by the increased risk for child maltreatment from domestic violence.

Other important factors that are taken into consideration in the family systems theory include family structure, styles of interaction, functions, roles, resources, family history, life cycles, and individual members. Family structure refers to the characteristics of its members, such as age, gender, the spacing of the children in ages, and the number of people in the family. Styles of interactions consist of the ways in which family members make decisions and solve problems. Family functions are the tasks that the family performs for its members and society, including economic, domestic, health care, socialization, reproduction, recreation, affection, self-identity, educational, and vocational functions (Turnbull et al., 1999).

Roles are the assigned responsibilities of the family members, such as the role of the household manager, the health caregiver, and the breadwinner. Family members can be assigned multiple roles. For example, one person could be the breadwinner and the household manager. Family resources include the health of its members, temperaments, social supports, skills, and financial supports. The history of the family consists of previous social and cultural experiences that affect and influence the ways that family members currently interpret events and feelings. The family life cycles are the changes or different stages that the family goes through beginning with courtship and ending with the deaths of the parents. Individual members are the people who compose the family. Each member has unique experiences outside the family that influence the inter-actions and behaviors of members within the family circle (Sattler, 1998; Turnbull et al., 1999).

Although the roles of teachers do not include directly interven-ing in family interactions, teachers still need to be aware of the whole family system when working with families that are at risk to stop child maltreatment. The teachers' understanding of the roles and functions of the family members can help them recognize the supports and resources they need to help the family members change and stop the maltreatment. An additional implication of the family systems theory is for teachers to realize that the interaction of mul-tiple stressors within the family, such as unemployment, poverty, lack of social supports, and ill health, could cause caregivers intense stress, reduce their quality and enjoyment of life, and heighten the risk that they will maltreat their children. If teachers assist the care-givers in gaining access to the necessary services, it is hoped that the children will benefit as well.

TEACHERS AS EFFECTIVE HELP GIVERS

To provide help effectively, teachers need to have constructive atti-tudes and nonpunitive approaches to families that are at risk for child maltreatment. Teachers can assist these families when they use the principles of family empowerment and by being sources of referral for necessary informal and formal supports and services (Dunst, Trivette, & Jodry, 1997).

Constructive and Nonpunitive Attitudes and Approaches

Constructive and nonpunitive attitudes approaches are necessary when teachers try to reach resistant family members. Even though it may be a natural tendency to regard caregivers who are abusive with hostility and a punitive attitude, it is more useful for teachers to think of them as human beings in need of therapeutic services and supports (Lowenthal, 1998). As a first step in the development of a constructive, nonpunitive approach and attitude, teachers should understand their own values, beliefs, and feelings about child mal-treatment and its prevention so that they can approach the care-givers who are abusive with nonjudgmental attitudes. It helps for teachers to remember that abuse is often intergenerational: Parents who are abusive probably are acting toward their children as they themselves were treated as children.

Although caregivers who are at risk may be resistant to the teachers' suggestions and consider them intrusive, they still desperately need assistance in increasing their self-worth and confidence (Berger, 1991). Caregivers who are at risk need supportive services, people on whom they can rely, and individuals who can be trusted to help meet their needs. Instead of criticism, the caregivers need reassurance that they can break their cycle of abuse or neglect by making necessary changes and obtaining appropriate supports and services. It is hoped that they will increase their self-esteem by developing more positive and meaningful relationships with their offspring and gaining the respect of other people. Because caregivers who are at risk may be unable to cope with their children, teachers need to be sources of referrals for them to appropriate mental health professionals and parenting programs that teach them coping skills without shaming them.

When teachers have nonpunitive attitudes, they are better able to establish partnerships with families that are at risk; communicate with openness and honesty; understand the needs of the families without prying into nonrelevant family activities; focus on solutions rather than causes or blame; emphasize behaviors that stop the maltreatment; and respect the confidentiality of the relationship except in cases of child maltreatment, which must be reported (Berger, 1991).

The Teacher's Role in Family Empowerment

Besides having nonpunitive and nonjudgmental attitudes, teachers can assist families that are at risk by using family empowerment or enablement principles (Dunst et al., 1997). Dunst et al. (1994) stated that when teachers empower and enable families, they create opportunities for families to feel more competent and independent in gaining access to needed supports and resources. Family members then gain a sense of being in control of their lives, which is often lacking in chaotic families that are at risk for child maltreatment. Another relevant principle of family empowerment is that every family has unique strengths and abilities. What one sees as poor functioning may be the result of a lack of supportive resources, which makes it impossible at the time for family members to demonstrate their strengths. When teachers provide information that assists the caregivers in acquiring needed supports, it is hoped that their child maltreatment will stop, their sense of well-being will increase, and their family functioning will be more appropriate.

Dunst et al. (1994) explained that the process of family empowerment requires a proactive stance by the help givers. Dunst et al. defined a *proactive stance* as a belief that all families are competent or capable of being competent. If teachers assume that families that are at risk are always incompetent and unable to change, then their assistance as educators is useless. The criteria necessary for teachers to take a proactive stance include providing enabling experiences and crediting positive changes to the actions of family members. Creating opportunities for the families to display their strengths is part of the teachers' responsibilities as help givers. An example is when teachers increase the pride of caregivers who are at risk by informing them about their children's many strengths. The caregivers feel more competent in their parenting skills and are less likely to abuse their children. The teachers can then attribute positive changes in parenting skills to the caregivers, which in turn may strengthen their self-esteem and feelings of being worthy in family matters. By using the principles of family empowerment, it is hoped that teachers can make their assistance to families that are at risk more meaningful and strengthen their rapport with them (McCollum & Yates, 1994).

THE IMPORTANCE OF INFORMAL AND FORMAL SUPPORTS

As help givers, teachers should assist families in identifying their needs and locating appropriate resources. When needs are met, they become resources for the family. Table 5.1 lists examples of family needs. The resources can consist of informal and formal supports. Informal supports can include people who help the family, such as extended family, friends, neighbors, co-workers, and organizations, such as social clubs, churches, and synagogues. Informal supports

Table 5.1. Family needs with examples

Needs	Examples
Financial	Enough money for basic needs
Basic necessities	Adequate place to live, food, and clothes
Health	Access to health care professionals
Employment	Job opportunities
Transportation	Ways to get places
Communication	Ways to get in touch with people
Education	Access to schools and further education
Child care	Babysitting and child care
Recreation	Access to places of recreation
Emotional/social	A feeling of caring and being accepted/participation in social clubs

Sources: Bennett, Lingerfelt, & Nelson (1990); Dunst, Trivette, & Deal (1994); Howard, Williams, Port, & Lepper (1997).

are usually easily available or can be made accessible to assist the family in everyday functioning. Professionals do not have to be contacted to obtain informal sources of support. Informal supports are not expensive, and professional expertise is not necessary.

In contrast, professionals and community agencies provide formal supports. Examples of these professionals include teachers, social workers, physicians, therapists, child care personnel, accountants, psychologists, and lawyers. Examples of community organizations include health departments and welfare agencies. Formal supports are more difficult to obtain than informal supports. They usually cost more, require technical expertise, and are often available only during regular working hours. Therefore, they should not be the only sources of support for families. Research has indicated that informal supports generally have more positive effects on the everyday functioning of families than formal ones and decrease the family members' stress (Dunst et al., 1994). Thus, it is important for teachers as help givers to assist families that are at risk in building systems of informal supports. These supports can help the caregivers make the necessary changes and stop their child maltreatment.

Bennett, Lingerfelt, and Nelson (1990) provided guidelines for professionals to assist families in identifying their informal supports and, if necessary, their formal ones. (See Figure 5.2 for examples of formal and informal family support.) The first guideline is to identify the family's personal networks by asking the family members to generate a list of people whom they see often and can be relied on to help. The second guideline is to determine who has previously helped the family members when necessary. The third guideline is to match the needs of the family with potential sources of support. This recommendation requires the teachers to first look within the family to see if any of its members can offer support. If this does not work, then they should look further into the family's potential network of supports. Eventually, the teachers' goals are to enable the family members to do this. The fourth guideline is to help find outside or more formal sources of support when needed. One way teachers can accomplish this is by setting up a meeting with the family members for the purpose of generating a list of professionals and relevant community organizations from the local telephone directory or to ask for recommendations from other people. The last guideline is to remove any obstacles that block the sources of support. An example is when a family member needs the services of a physician. Referrals can be made, but if the family lacks transportation, then the teacher can help think of ways to get

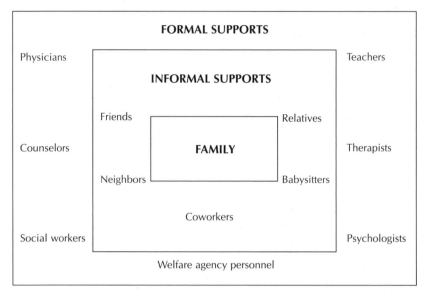

Figure 5.2. Examples of formal and informal family supports. (*Sources:* Bennett, Lingerfelt, & Nelson [1990]; Dunst, Trivette, & Deal [1994]; Howard, Williams, Port, & Lepper [1997].)

to the appointment, such as using public transportation or asking friends for rides in exchange for babysitting.

When following these guidelines, teachers can focus on the following tips given by Bennett et al. (1990):

- First, look within the family for resources. Help should be obtained as much as possible at the family level and then through the informal network of supports.
- Second, do not use formal supports if informal ones will meet the family's needs.
- Third, use formal supports if no satisfactory informal resources can be found.
- Fourth, encourage the family members to be as independent as possible in identifying and contacting their sources of support.
- Fifth, create other opportunities for family members to feel empowered by practicing their new skills of generating and identifying their supports and services.

COMMUNICATION SKILLS

Communication skills are especially essential when family members are at risk because they may be resistant and hard to reach.

Communication skills include active listening, effective questioning, and the appropriate use of expanded and closed statements (Cook et al., 1996; Crais, 1996; Howard, Williams, Port, & Lepper, 1997).

Active Listening

The skill of active listening is important in building rapport with family members, as it encourages them to communicate and conveys the teachers' feelings of concern for them. This skill includes the use of minimal encouragements, reflection of feelings, clarification of responses, paraphrasing, and summarizing. Minimal encouragements are the use of verbal expressions and body language that let the speakers know that the listeners are paying attention to what is being said. Some examples of verbal minimal encouragements include expressions such as "Hmmm," "Please continue," or "I would like to hear more." An example of minimal encouragements through the use of body language is when the listener establishes appropriate eye contact and leans forward to listen more.

Reflection of feelings occurs when the listeners communicate their understanding of the feelings of the speakers and the willingness to be corrected if they are misperceived. An example of this skill is when a teacher perceives that a parent appears uneasy or troubled about an event. To reflect this feeling, the teacher may say, "You seem to be upset about what happened." Clarification of responses is used when the listener is not sure of what the speaker said and asks for it to be repeated. Paraphrasing happens when the listener reflects on the content of the speaker's conversations and then paraphrases what has been said. Summarizing occurs when the listener offers periodic summaries of previous conversations, which again gives the speaker chances to correct any misunderstandings (Howard et al., 1997).

Effective Questioning

Effective questioning occurs when the teacher as the speaker asks open-ended questions to obtain more information rather than questions that can be answered with a "yes" or a "no," although these types of questions can be beneficial when more precise information is needed. When opening a conversation, Winton (1996) recommended asking the open-ended questions because they allow the listener to then talk about what is significant to him or her. Her other recommendations are to avoid asking questions that begin with "why" because they tend to make the listener feel defensive, keep questions simple and ask only one at a time, ask questions in order to communicate interest in the listener and the topic of conversation rather than questions that attempt to judge or analyze, and emphasize questions that convey an interest in past positive events and activities of the family so that their strengths can begin to be identified (Winton, 1996).

Expanded and Closed Statements

Howard et al. (1997) advocated for the use of expanded statements rather than closed statements by speakers. Expanded statements encourage further conversations, whereas closed statements have the effect of shutting off any further discussions. When teachers are skilled in making expanded statements, family members who are at risk have more opportunity to discuss their concerns. Howard et al. (1997) provided the following examples of the different types of closed statements:

1. One type of closed statement occurs when the speaker provides direct advice and persuasion (e.g., "If I were in your place, I would not do it").
2. The second kind of closed statement occurs when the speaker changes the subject without explaining the reason.
3. The third type of closed statement occurs when the speaker holds the listener to the future (e.g., "I'm sure you will see I'm right later on").
4. The fourth type of closed statements occurs when the speaker denies the feelings of the listener (e.g., "You really don't feel that way, do you?").
5. The fifth type of closed statement is when the speaker tries to control the listener by using shame (e.g., "You should be ashamed of yourself and very sorry that you did this").

Teachers who want family members to feel free to discuss their views and opinions should avoid closed statements. Some closed statements are described as "killers" by Howard et al. (1997) because they choke off or "kill" any further conversation. Some examples of "killer" closed statements include the following: "It sounds like a good solution but. . . ." "We'll never have the money," "We never did it this way before," "There just isn't time to do it," "No one is ready to do this," and "You must have a better plan, because this one will never work." As stated previously, teachers need to use expanded statements when communicating with families that are at risk because these statements convey to the family members the teachers' respect for their feelings and their encouragement for them to talk openly about their concerns.

SENSITIVITY TO FAMILY DIVERSITIES

Another value of effective communication skills is being able to reach and assist caregivers who are at risk and their children who have diverse backgrounds. American families are becoming increasingly diverse. In order to help all families, teachers need to be sensitive to these diversities and be aware of cultural and age issues. The issues discussed in this section include awareness of one's own culture, the differences in family structures, diverse child-rearing practices, different perspectives about the etiology of children's disabilities, diverse medical practices, and diverse approaches to child discipline. At the end of this section, the need for culturally responsive training for teachers is emphasized.

Awareness of One's Own Culture

Awareness of one's own culture is a first step in recognizing the cultural diversity of others. Teachers should examine their own beliefs and attitudes toward race, cultures, linguistic differences, and family structures. Many Anglo Americans believe in the value of personal autonomy, independence, self-help, control of one's life, individual achievement, equality, and informality in their relationships with people (Au & Kawakami, 1991). It is easy to assume that these values are the same in individuals from other cultures. Their beliefs, however, could be very different. For example, Native Americans are judged by their contributions to the group and the community rather than by their individual achievements (Vaughn, Bos, & Schumm, 2000). Conflict and a sense of mistrust could result if teachers are unaware that the values of the families with whom they are working are different than their own. If cultural differences are not taken into account, then the assistance proposed by teachers may be considered inappropriate and resisted by the families.

Differences in Family Structures

In some families of diverse cultural backgrounds, extended family members are the primary caregivers (Phillips, 1994). The elders can play significant roles in decision making and child care. Native American children may view grandparents, aunts, uncles, and older siblings as additional parents (Bearcrane, Dodd, Nelson, & Ostwald, 1990). Hispanic, Asian, and African American families often are committed to the value of the extended family and the idea of working together to achieve group goals (Groce & Zola, 1993; Lynch, 1998).

Awareness of the family structure can help eliminate misunderstandings about child maltreatment among teachers and family members. For example, parental neglect would not be shown in extended families in which the other family members are responsible for the care of children. The teacher needs to learn who the primary caregivers are in the family that is at risk and involve all of them in making the decisions about necessary services and appropriate interventions.

Child-Rearing Practices

In Anglo American families, children often are expected to be as independent as possible. Child-rearing practices reflect this viewpoint in that they stress early toilet training, weaning, self-reliance, and early readiness for school. In some families from diverse backgrounds, however, dependence is expected in childhood. For example, in traditional Cuban cultures, there is the fear that if too much independence is stressed, children will be at risk for physical harm. Therefore, toddlers are not encouraged to crawl or walk early. Also, there is a belief that the mother's role is to remain at home and create a strong bond with her children, which often promotes feelings of dependency in the children. From this cultural perspective, autonomy in children could be a sign of poor parenting (DeSantis & Thomas, 1994). The American goals of autonomy and assertiveness may be seen as disrespectful in Cuban children.

In contrast, traditional Haitian beliefs encourage independence, and children are trained to be self-reliant and self-sufficient (Glasgow & Adaskin, 1990). Young children help with the household chores. Girls of preschool age may be expected to help sell food at the market. Boys may assist with farming and taking care of cattle. Although independence is stressed and expected in children, they also are trained to be obedient and subordinate to authority figures.

It is essential to remember, however, that each family is unique, and general characteristics are not applicable to all members of a particular culture. Other factors also can influence the child-rearing practices of families from diverse backgrounds, such as the amount of time spent in the United States, the level of education, their experiences, and the degree of acculturation or how much the family members identify with their original culture. In addition, differences can exist between these members as to appropriate ways to raise their children. Therefore, to effectively assist families that are at risk in preventing child maltreatment, teachers need to learn the specific child-rearing values and practices of the individual caregivers (Beckman, 1996).

Diversity in Perspectives About the Etiology
of Children's Disabilities and the Values of Intervention

The ways in which families from different cultures perceive the etiology of disabilities is of significance as it affects their attitudes toward their children with special needs. A disability can be viewed by some cultures as a form of punishment (Groce & Zola, 1993). Some people believe that a child with a disability and his or her family is cursed by God and that the disability is a punishment for past sins. Support for the family members is minimal as people in the community may try to distance themselves from the "evil" family. The caregivers may blame their children with special needs for their social isolation, become angry, and be at risk for child maltreatment. A number of African and Caribbean societies believe that witchcraft is responsible for disabilities (Groce, 1990). Therefore, an individual who has a disability is thought to be bewitched. A version of this belief in some Latin American families is that the disability is caused by the *mal ojo* or the evil eye. Close association with a child with disabilities is thought to put others at risk for witchcraft and curses. Hereditary disorders may be seen by some societies as being caused by a curse or "bad blood." In traditional Southeast Asian groups, a disability may be perceived as evidence for a transgression committed in a previous life (Chan, 1998). The child with the disability may be avoided and socially isolated. The responsibility for the disability as well as its cure is placed on the child and his or her family.

The consequences of these beliefs can affect how families treat their children with disabilities. Family members may feel ashamed and, therefore, may neglect these children. This neglect may take the form of being too embarrassed to accept the help of the teacher in obtaining the needed services. Keeping the child isolated at home, unseen by others, may be a way of coping with the disability. Even when family members are aware of the need for interventions to assist the child, they can be reluctant to accept them because of the fear of being disgraced when the disability is publicly known. Other families, such as those of traditional Vietnamese cultures, may have a fatalistic view of the disability and believe their children with disabilities cannot benefit from the services. In contrast, some Hispanic groups believe that children with disabilities are gifts from God and should be cherished and protected and, therefore, services and interventions are not considered necessary (Lequerica, 1993).

To better serve diverse families that have children with disabilities, it is essential for teachers to understand the perceptions the families may have about the causes of the disabilities and the value of interventions. The stress and discrimination the family members may incur can put them at risk for child maltreatment. These families deserve clear explanations in their own languages of the interventions and services proposed for them and their children. They need to know why they are necessary and how they can participate in partnership with the professionals in making culturally sensitive decisions.

Diversity of Communication Styles

There are two concerns in communicating clearly with families from diverse cultural and linguistic backgrounds that are at risk. One concern is the use of interpreters, and the other concern is the recognition of different interaction styles. When using interpreters to assist in cross-cultural communications, teachers must keep in mind that the words used in conversations with others can be misunderstood when interpreters translate them into other languages. The author of this book experienced this when she used the word *collaborator* in talking about the value of a team partnership to Russian educators who had recently arrived in the United States. They appeared uncomfortable when the word was translated into Russian because they interpreted "collaborator" to be a member of the Russian secret police.

If interpreters are available to assist teachers, they should have the following skills and abilities: proficiency in the language spoken by the family members and the teachers, the ability to explain diverse values and traditions, proficiency in cross-cultural communication, and the ability to keep information confidential (Hanson & Lynch, 1992). Lynch (1998) suggested that ideal interpreters are culturally sensitive informants who can explain diverse customs, beliefs, and styles of communication to school personnel.

Teachers also need skills to work successfully with interpreters when communicating with families that are at risk. Prior to the first meeting with the family, the teacher should convey to the interpreter the main purpose of the meeting and the issues that will be discussed. During the family interview, the teacher needs to directly address his or her remarks to the family members rather than to the interpreter. In addition, it is important that the teacher correctly pronounce the names of the family members. The teacher can show respect for the family by using a positive tone of voice and facial expression and by avoiding any offensive body language. Between translations, the teacher should limit his or her remarks and questions so as not to overwhelm the family and the interpreter. In addition, if possible, relevant printed materials in the family members' own language can be given to them to read (Lynch, 1998).

Another issue in cross-cultural communication is that different cultures can have diverse interaction styles. There are cultures that emphasize that children are to be seen but not heard. Behaviors such as talking assertively to adults or making direct eye contact with them are regarded as disrespectful and unmannerly. These behaviors can put the children at risk for discipline in the form of physical punishment. Turning the eyes downward to the speaker implies one is listening intently in some Asian, African, and Native American societies (Williams, 1994). Asian children may be cautioned not to ask questions of authority figures. Questioning in this case is thought to be disrespectful (Chan, 1998). The teacher needs to be aware that some Asian parents may smile and nod as if they agree with what is being proposed. These actions, however, are to show respect to the professionals and not necessarily to show agreement.

Differences in interaction styles also can be reflected in the length of time that it takes to build relationships with family members. Some families focus on long-term relationships and want to know the teachers better through many visits (Allen & Majidi-Ahi, 1989). Anglo Americans tend to be informal in their interactions and want to establish quick relationships with professionals. Some cultures may be direct in their communications, whereas others prefer an indirect style in expressing their wishes. In many societies, there are differences in communication involving personal space, eye contact, wait time, tone of voice, facial expressions, and touching, which teachers need to comprehend to work effectively with families that are at risk from diverse cultural-linguistic backgrounds (Salend & Taylor, 1993).

Diversity in Approaches to Discipline

Different approaches to child discipline can be observed in diverse cultures. In American society, there is a stress on the democratic style of discipline, which avoids corporal punishment and gives the children the right to explain the reasons for their misbehaviors (Harry, 1992). In some Native American cultures, children are given the same respect and rights as adults. The children are praised for group cooperation and for fulfilling responsibilities without being asked (Joe & Malach, 1998). The philosophy of child discipline in these cultures stresses that children will behave appropriately if adults first model the appropriate behaviors.

In other societies, there may be more authoritative approaches to discipline (Hildebrand, Phenice, Gray, & Hines, 2000). In some cultures, the father is regarded as the absolute authority and uses corporal punishment when he believes that it is necessary to obtain child compliance and respect. In this philosophy of child discipline, signs of good parenting are seen in caregivers who take care not to spoil their children and who physically punish their children for disobedience. A saying that could characterize this type of discipline is "Spare the rod and spoil the child." In this case, the teacher who is culturally responsive, after listening to and understanding the perspective of the caregiver, needs to point out that in America, too harsh punishment is regarded as abuse. Other, more positive methods of child discipline, which encourage respect and dignity for themselves and their offspring can be explained to the parents.

Diversity in Medical Practices

Medical practices in some cultures may mimic physical maltreatment of children. For example, in some families of Asian heritage, common treatments for colds and body aches include coining, spooning, cupping, and moxibustion (Sattler, 1998). Coining involves applying a medicated ointment and then gently rubbing the area with the edge of a coin. The rubbing makes dark marks on the skin that look like bruises (Chan, 1998). When spooning is practiced, water or a saline solution is rubbed on the back, neck, shoulders, chest, or forehead. Then the area is pinched until it reddens and scratched with a porcelain spoon until superficial bruises are seen. Cupping involves the burning of a material in a cup, which is then placed on the painful area. This procedure leaves circular burns on the skin. Moxibustion involves burning a moxa plant and then placing it near the sore body part. This treatment creates tiny craters on the skin. The bruises and burns that appear from these treatments usually disappear within a short time. They can, however, easily be thought of as physical maltreatment. A number of physicians have stated that there are no medical reasons to stop these treatments because the injuries are superficial (Chan, 1998). Because they are often confused with abuse, however, the family members who practice them can be accused of child maltreatment. Opportunities for cross-cultural discussions between the teachers and caregivers should be encouraged so that the families understand how the mainstream culture may view these treatments as abuse (Chao, 1992).

The Need for Culturally Responsive Training

Teachers can increase their awareness and sensitivity to these diversities through culturally responsive training. This training can further the goals of communicating with and reaching families that are at risk. As of 2001, the number of well-trained bilingual and culturally responsive teachers is small compared with the increasing number of diverse families in need of services. The preparation of teachers from diverse cultures is a priority. Until this happens, however, Anglo American teachers will, for the most part, continue to provide these services. A majority of these professionals will need specific training to be successful in forming partnerships with caregivers from diverse backgrounds.

The following competencies have been identified as being necessary for teachers in their training (Chan, 1998; Joe & Malach, 1998):

1. Teachers need to be cognizant of their own cultures, beliefs, values, and practices and need to analyze how these have influenced their lifestyles.
2. The cultures of the families must be understood for effective communication with them. Identifying similarities between their values and those of the teachers while acknowledging and respecting the differences will be helpful.
3. It is important to recognize that every family, regardless of its cultural, linguistic, or ethnic heritage, is unique in its ways of functioning and in its degree of identification with a particular culture. Teachers need to keep in mind both the individual families as well as their common cultural backgrounds when assisting family members who are at risk.
4. Teachers should know how to gain information from resource people in the community to better understand the families' values and traditions.
5. Teachers should be familiar with ways to empower diverse families that are at risk to gain access to resources and support networks. The resources must meet the needs of the individual family to better enable the caregivers to stop their child maltreatment.
6. Cultural responsiveness to the concerns and strengths of each family is a necessary competency for school personnel.
7. Knowledge of family systems and diverse family structures can further bicultural competence.

To assist teachers in acquiring these competencies, more university programs should include coursework in the following areas: family systems theories, diverse family structures, styles of communication, service coordination, teamwork with other professionals and families, and ethnic-cultural diversity. The practica for students need to incorporate direct experiences in forming partnerships with families that are at risk, service providers, and professionals from diverse cultures. In addition, relevant in-service workshops, experiences, and consultations with individuals from diverse cultures can assist teachers already working at schools.

DIVERSITY IN AGES

This last section focuses on the issues of very young caregivers, many of whom are unmarried mothers (Lowenthal & Lowenthal, 1997). These single teenage mothers often have multiple stressors, which can put them at risk for maltreating their children. In order to assist them, it is important to understand the challenges that they and their children face and which interventions may be helpful (Hildebrand et al., 2000).

Challenges for Adolescent Mothers

Handling the dramatic changes of adolescence is difficult enough. Mastering the developmental tasks of adolescence and becoming a parent at the same time is especially demanding. These two tasks can easily conflict with each other, meaning that a teenage mother often will compromise one role or fail at both (Lowenthal & Lowenthal, 1997). Adolescent parenthood can be described as an "off time" in the transition to adulthood (Boxer, 1992). By becoming parents, teenagers disrupt the expected sequence of first, finishing school; second, finding employment; next, marrying; and last, having children. Many teenage parents feel socially isolated because it can be difficult to find friends that share parenting experiences.

Adolescents' typical self-absorption makes it difficult to distinguish their children's needs from their own. Indeed, teenage mothers are usually still emotionally dependent on their own mothers. In addition, adolescents may have unrealistic expectations about child development (Musick, 1994), which may lead to child abuse when those expectations are not realized. Compared with older women, adolescent mothers are more impatient and punitive and less nurturing (Cooper, Dunst, & Vance, 1990). They may also be so stressed by the challenges of motherhood that they become depressed, develop poor self-esteem, and are not able to provide their children with emotional stability.

Other attendant risks of adolescent motherhood are an inability to make appropriate decisions because of a lack of experience, greater health risks during pregnancy because of poor prenatal care, a tendency for prolonged and difficult labor, a lack of social support systems, and an inability to handle financial matters. Teenage mothers often find it difficult to prioritize financial needs (e.g., when to pay the doctors, how to pay for food, how to obtain money for medicine). Also, families headed by teenage parents are more likely to live in poverty (Unger & Cooley, 1992).

Other negative consequences of early childbearing can include dropping out of school because of parenting responsibilities, having limited vocational skills, having additional pregnancies, and being homeless as a result of poverty. It has been estimated that 17% of teenage mothers will be pregnant again within 1 year, and 30% will have more children within 2 years (Summerlin, 1990). Having more children can cause further financial and socioemotional stresses. Furthermore, the salary that a teenage mother can be expected to earn over her lifetime is half that of someone who delays childbearing (Summerlin, 1990). Because of economic reasons, many adolescent mothers and their children are homeless. They may live in temporary shelters that are overcrowded and noisy, lack privacy, and offer limited opportunities for nurturing parent–child interactions (Anderson & Koblinsky, 1995).

Challenges for the Children of Teenage Parents

Children of teenage parents face additional challenges of their own. Teenagers are twice as likely to have premature infants compared with mothers who are in their 20s (Tyree, Vance, & Boals, 1991). Low birth weight infants are 40 times more likely to die during their first month of life when compared with infants of normal weights. In addition, health problems and disabilities are 39% higher in low birth weight premature infants (Tyree et al., 1991).

Another serious concern is the connection among teenage parenting, child maltreatment, and poverty. As previously mentioned, for a number of reasons, maltreatment is more likely when the family lives in poverty, which is common in households headed by teenage parents (Hegar & Scannapieco, 1995). Child neglect, also a serious problem in families headed by teenage parents, is responsible for even more deaths than child abuse. Child neglect can occur because of the typical self-absorption of adolescence in which teenage parents may be unaware of and not provide for the basic survival needs of their children, such as appropriate food, shelter, clothing, health care, and protection from danger. Children who survive child neglect when they are young are at risk for physical and mental disabilities as they get older (Summerlin, 1990).

It is estimated that families headed by young, single mothers represent a large majority of homeless people (Anderson & Koblinsky, 1995). To add to their plight, homeless children are likely to suffer from emotional difficulties, such as depression and aggression, and are at greater risk for such health problems as asthma, anemia, and infections. Because homeless families headed by single parents are often transient, many children cannot regularly attend school and will need special education services. All of these factors can put the children of single, adolescent parents at risk for abuse.

Interventions for Teenage Parents and Their Young Children

A number of interventions are available to assist teenage parents and their children (Hamburg & Dixon, 1992; Tyree et al., 1991), including programs that provide pregnancy prevention information, counseling, life skills training, educational and vocational preparation, prenatal care and parenting education, and appropriate child care and social support systems. Preventing pregnancy is the first intervention. Adolescents need to be educated about the consequences of being sexually active and the importance of delaying childbearing. Through counseling, adolescents can learn about prevention and receive the encouragement they may need to finish school. Teachers can be sources of referral for these counselors and also can help identify resources for health care, life skills training (e.g., financial and household management), housing, welfare payments, and social support (e.g., extended family, neighbors, friends).

The Benefits of Parenting Programs

Teenage parents, as well as other caregivers who are at risk, can benefit from parenting programs to which teachers may lead or refer them. The goals of these programs include increasing the caregivers' knowledge of child development, appropriate expectations of children, and positive methods of discipline (Reppucci et al., 1997). Research has indicated that a number of cases of child maltreatment occur because of inappropriate expectations of children (Altepeter & Walker, 1992). Caregivers can misinterpret the noncompliance of the children who have developmental limitations as intentional defiance and misbehavior. Caregivers who are at risk may then resort to harsh punishment and maltreatment to gain compliance. Parent education programs seek to deter this maltreatment by having discussions about child development and appropriate expectations. Caregivers who were mistreated themselves as children also benefit from the more positive modeling of child-rearing skills and discipline strategies advocated by these programs.

Selected examples of parenting programs that teachers can lead are the Systematic Training for Effective Parenting (STEP) Program (Dinkmeyer & McKay, 1989), Parent Effectiveness Training (Gordon, 1975), and the Active Parenting Program (Popkin, 1989). The STEP Program consists of lectures and discussions about parenting skills and emphasizes communication skills and basic counseling techniques. The STEP Program, published by American Guidance Service in Circle Pines, Minnesota, consists of 2-hour training sessions, once a week for 9 weeks, which guide parents to relate more positively with their children by identifying the goals of their behaviors. Cassettes and clearly written parent and leadership manuals are provided. The leadership manuals are easy for teachers to follow and contain all of the information needed to conduct the sessions. Studies of the STEP Program indicate that the parent participants became more democratic in their parenting practices, encouraged more verbalizations from their children, were less likely to use harsh punishments, and were more able to understand their children's behaviors based on their knowledge of child development (Allan, 1994; Dinkmeyer, McKay, & Dinkmeyer, 1990).

The Parent Effectiveness Training Program, which is published by Wyden Press, located in New York, New York, discusses the following topics: the power of active listening for caregivers, changing children's behaviors through modifications in their environments, and the "no-lose" method of solving parent–child conflicts in which positive methods of discipline are emphasized.

The Active Parent Program stresses active listening and communication skills, alternatives to physical punishment, family discussion, and the use of natural and logical consequences as methods of positive discipline for children. Parent and group leader manuals are provided that give explicit examples and strategies (Popkin, 1989). The leader manuals could be effective tools for teachers who wish to conduct the sessions. The Active Parent Program is published by Academic Press, located in San Diego, California.

All three programs include intervention techniques and ideas useful for teachers when they assist families that are at risk and their children. Information about these programs can be obtained from the publishers.

CONCLUSION

This chapter has discussed ways that teachers can assist and inter-vene with families who are at risk for child maltreatment. Chapter 7 focuses on other kinds of interventions. These are suggested for teachers to implement when assisting their students who are at risk in the social-emotional and behavioral areas of development.

7

SOCIAL SKILL STRATEGIES
AND INTERVENTIONS

This chapter examines strategies and socioemotional interventions that make classrooms safe, predictable, and nurturing environments for children who are maltreated. The strategies provide structure using consistent routines, reasonable rules and limits, appropriate methods of discipline, behavioral supports, natural and logical consequences, and other techniques of behavior management. This chapter also discusses a variety of socioemotional interventions consisting of general instruction in social skills and specific training in the development of friendships, recognition of and appropriate expression of feelings and emotions, anger control, conflict management, development of an internal sense of control, and ways to foster self-esteem. These particular skills were selected because of their importance to many children who are maltreated. The most significant socioemotional intervention, however, is the teacher. The teacher has many opportunities to make an important and positive impact on the lives of these children who are maltreated and can be a facilitator of resiliency for these students (Weinreb, 1997).

STRATEGIES FOR BUILDING SAFE
AND PREDICTABLE CLASSROOM ENVIRONMENTS

A number of children who are maltreated may have chaotic home environments, which can produce pervasive anxiety and anger in them. These emotions may be reflected in disruptive behaviors at school. Children who are maltreated can benefit from very structured and predictable schedules and routines because these tend to increase feelings of safety and security. Routines can be reinforced through daily activities (Cook, Tessier, & Klein, 2000). Visual aids, such as pictures, photographs, charts, and signs, act as reminders of class schedules along with verbal explanations. It is helpful if teachers refer to the periods during the day by name (e.g., group time, recess, center time) and indicate what is expected at each time. Then, at the end of each period, they can review what has occurred and discuss what will happen next. Reviewing necessary changes at the beginning of the day prepares the students and avoids possible frustration and temper tantrums later.

Children who are maltreated need teachers who are emotionally stable and predictable. It is essential for these children to know that their teachers are in control of themselves because it is frightening for the children to feel that their school caregivers are disorganized, confused, or anxious. Of course, teachers are not expected to be perfect, but when they are upset, they need to inform the students of the reasons for their distress and reassure them that they will soon feel better (Ferber, 1996).

Transitions often are difficult for children. Children who are neglected and abused and who are unsure of the availability of their family caregivers may regard transitions as especially frightening because they increase their insecurity. To prepare students for making the transition to the next activity, signals can be given, such as flicking the lights, playing a note on the piano, or singing a special song. The children need time to disengage from activities just as they need time to get involved in them. The following are other suggestions for teachers that will help all children adjust to transitions (Cole, 1995; Cook et al., 2000):

- Limit the number of transitions by streamlining the class schedule.
- Provide explanations as often as needed about the reasons for the changes.
- Decrease the waiting times when some of the children are through with an activity and are waiting for their classmates to finish. Misbehavior is more likely to occur at these times. To prevent this, the teacher should have some simple activities available, such as self-selected books and board games.
- Have the materials for the next activity set up and ready to use, which also decreases waiting times.

The physical needs of the children should be kept in mind to enable them to pay attention to school tasks (Berger, 2000). Accommodations to these needs require the teacher to notice and care for signs of hunger, fatigue, thirst, and toileting needs. In scheduling, teacher-led activities need to be alternated with child-initiated ones, and quiet activities balanced with active ones. The teacher should also alternate individual work with small- and large-group assignments. The teacher should help excitable students calm down by modeling deep breathing, counting to 10, and self-talk. An orderly, organized, and neat physical environment also can have a calming effect. Therefore, broken equipment should be fixed or removed, and there should be specific places for books, games, toys, and classroom materials (Cole, 1995).

Other suggestions for teachers that help make school an emotionally and physically safe place include giving the students choices; setting achievable goals; protecting them from disturbing noises and distractions; and offering opportunities for the children to participate in creative activities, such as art, music, and drama. Children who are maltreated may lack a sense of control in their home lives. When given choices at school, their sense of being in control is facilitated as well as their feelings of safety and security. Setting attainable goals increases students' self-confidence, especially when they receive sincere praise for their efforts. They may rarely receive such compliments at home. To lengthen their attention span for school tasks, teachers should avoid auditory and visual distractions when possible, such as overcrowded classes and loud noises. Participation in creative work, such as in art, music, and drama, gives children who are abused and neglected the freedom and safety to express their feelings in constructive ways. Participation in after-school extracurricular activities provides a safe haven for these children who come from abusive and neglectful homes and may decrease possible delinquency and unsafe behaviors (Koplow, 1996).

THE NECESSITY FOR REASONABLE RULES AND LIMITS

Another method of enhancing a sense of security is to establish consistent rules and clear limits. Because some children who are maltreated have caregivers who exert authority in frightening ways, it is essential that rules be established within a nurturing, supportive relationship with the teacher. When rules or limits are set in a neutral, consistent, and meaningful manner, these children can learn to trust and develop their confidence that adults can be authoritative without being hurtful or threatening. They need to know that their teachers can say "no" but that they are still available to assist and guide them. It is hoped that these children will then be motivated to follow the rules and to tolerate frustration without acting out in inappropriate behaviors (Ferber, 1996).

In order for rules to be reasonable, they should be developmentally appropriate in their expectations. For example, kindergarten children should not have a rule that they must always sit quietly in their seats during every activity. Developmentally, their attention spans are limited, and they need times when they can be active and exercise their motor skills. Reasonable rules will provide the structure for acceptable behaviors. Only rules that are necessary for a positive learning environment should be established. In addition, limits are best adhered to when they are collaboratively derived by both the students and teachers. When the rules and limits need modifications, both parties should be involved in making the changes. When developing rules, the following advice is beneficial (Vaughn, Bos, & Schumm, 2000): 1) Students are more likely to follow rules if they are generously praised for their efforts, and 2) rules need to be stated in positive ways. Some examples of general classroom rules are provided by Bos and Vaughn (1998) and Ferber (1996):

1. No one can be hurt by others.
2. No property can be destroyed without permission.
3. All assignments must be completed on time.

APPROPRIATE METHODS OF DISCIPLINE

Children who are maltreated may need several types of discipline methods that are appropriate to meet their needs (Cicchetti, Toth, & Hennessy, 1989). Children who are physically abused can misinterpret their peers' playful behaviors as threatening and anxiety provoking. As a result, they may lash out with verbal and physical aggression. Children who are severely neglected may treat other children as objects and grab their toys and food. Other students who are at risk for maltreatment may display negative behaviors in order to get the attention that they are severely lacking at home. If a teacher responds to and disciplines all of these children in the same way, their individual needs will not be met and their behavior difficulties may worsen.

Teachers, with the help of counselors, social workers, and psychologists, should try to understand the underlying reasons for the negative behaviors. Aggressive students who are maltreated need to learn how to better interpret the emotions and actions of others and recognize their own feelings as well. They must learn how to positively communicate with other people. Suggestions for teachers about ways to build these skills are provided in the section of this chapter titled "Training in Selected Social Skills." Discipline should be firm but neutral. In addition, the teacher must demonstrate the social advantages of positive behaviors, which help children make friends with other students. Children who are abused and neglected are often anxious and fearful; they should be kept busy with school activities and be given appropriate choices so that they feel more in control over what happens to them. Punishment, although it should be avoided if at all possible, should be brief and mild if necessary (Cicchetti et al., 1989; Ferber, 1996; Koplow, 1996).

In addition, it is essential that punishment not be combined with positive regard or affection for these students. Many of them receive confusing messages from their caregivers. For example, a parent could be abusive one moment and overly affectionate the next minute in order to obtain the child's compliance. Therefore, the teacher should not use a confusing method of discipline, such as removing the child from an activity while expressing a positive feeling by saying, "You know how much I care for you." Coercion and power struggles need to be avoided. The emphasis should be on praise and positive reinforcement, as much as possible, through the recognition of the child's efforts, strengths, successes, and interests (Lowenthal, 1996).

THE USE OF NATURAL AND LOGICAL CONSEQUENCES

Natural and logical consequences represent an alternate type of approach to discipline that can assist some children who are maltreated in acquiring more appropriate behaviors. This method of discipline is derived from Adlerian philosophy, which believes that children learn from their behaviors when offered safe, natural, and logical consequences (Adler, 1964; Dinkmeyer & McKay, 1989). Natural consequences happen when an adult does not interfere, and the children learn from what happens after their inappropriate behaviors. For example, if children who are maltreated refuse to cooperatively play a game, their peers will probably avoid playing with them next time. Natural consequences must be used only when they are safe alternatives. For example, a young child should not be allowed to burn her hand in order to remember not to touch the hot stove.

Logical consequences are those that do not naturally happen but are arranged by an adult (Marion, 1999). These consequences are called logical because of their logical relationships to the misbehavior. In order for a consequence to be associated with a specific behavior, it must be immediate so that the child will remember the cause and effect. At school, the use of logical consequences can assist children who are maltreated in understanding the reasons for being disciplined. For example, if a child destroys classroom materials and temporarily is denied their use, she can better understand how her actions brought about the punishment than if she was placed in a time-out chair. The logical consequence assists her in focusing on how to change her behavior for the better. It also gives her an opportunity to make appropriate choices in her behaviors the next time (Cook et al., 2000).

BEHAVIORAL SUPPORTS

Behavioral supports "emphasize the use of a collaborative problem-solving process to develop individualized interventions that stress the prevention of problem behaviors through the provision of effective educational programming" (Snell & Janney, 2000, p. 2). To be effective, this approach necessitates teaching the student appropriate behaviors that can be substituted for negative ones (Taylor, 2000). Janney and Snell (2000) described some characteristics of behavioral supports that make them especially appealing when assisting children with disruptive behaviors who have been maltreated:

- Positive behavioral supports are respectful. They do not use force, cause pain, or cause emotional distress. They emphasize caring and trusting relationships with students.
- Behavioral supports can be used in inclusive environments in both public and private schools. They give the students who are at risk for maltreatment chances to work with, play with, and learn more appropriate behaviors from the modeling of some peers who have more appropriate social skills. Better ways of coping and problem solving can be demonstrated to them in an incidental manner.
- Behavioral supports stress the avoidance of failure. These supports focus on successful self-management procedures and the ability to express feelings in appropriate ways. This is a necessary positive emphasis for children who are at risk with disruptive behaviors.
- Behavioral supports focus on teaching social skills for successful interpersonal relationships, not just on controlling behavior.
- Behavioral supports are individualized to meet the unique needs of the student. An individualized behavior support plan (IBSP) is developed and monitored for its success in improving the target behavior.

Teachers can implement a number of behavioral supports including 1) modifying the curriculum to simplify it or to include more functional, adaptive, or social skills; 2) providing accommodations, such as additional tutoring; 3) arranging preferential seating in close proximity to the teacher; 4) assigning a peer buddy to help with difficult classwork and to model more positive social skills; 5) providing easy access to school mental health professionals, such as psychologists, counselors, and social workers; and 6) alternating easy with difficult subjects and balancing quiet with busy times (Bos & Vaughn, 1998; Farmer, Farmer, & Gut, 1999; Janney & Snell, 2000). Behavioral supports also respect individual choices, emphasize appropriate social skills, and promote success in everyday interactions. Perhaps most beneficial, behavioral supports stress caring, empathetic relationships between teachers and their students within the context of encouraging more positive behaviors.

The Development of an Individualized Support Plan (ISP)

The development of a functional behavioral assessment plan is required by school personnel in the Individuals with Disabilities Education Act (IDEA) Amendments of 1997, PL 105-17, for a child who is removed from school for more than 10 school days for behavior problems. It can be a voluntary option, however, for any child who exhibits troubling behaviors. The functional behavioral assessment plan is also referred to as an ISP (Taylor, 2000).

There is a sequence of steps in the development of an ISP. The first step is to objectively define the problem behavior and the purpose it serves (Taylor, 2000). There are many possible purposes or intents for behaviors, including power or control, avoidance or escape, acceptance or belonging, self-expression, attention, reward, and revenge or justice (Taylor, 2000). When defining the purpose, specific and observable terminology must be used. For example, instead of the teacher saying that the child is aggressive, it is important to state exactly what occurred (e.g., "Mary hit Billy with her fist five times during the 10-minute reading period"). If a student displays more than one problem behavior, priorities have to be established. Destructive behaviors, such as hurting oneself or others, are the first priority for an ISP. The second priority is disruptive behavior, such as temper tantrums. The third and least priority is distracting actions, such as tearing papers or books.

The second step in the development of an ISP involves gathering information about the student in order to understand better the intent of the behavior. Information concerning the student's home and school environments is collected. Relevant questions are asked, such as "How is the child's home life? Who are his or her care-givers? What events occur at school before the target behavior, or what are its antecedents? What is the exact environment? Who is there, and when does it happen? How often does it happen? What happens after the behavior, or what are its consequences?" (Horner & Carr, 1997).

In the third step, a hypothesis is developed, which relates the antecedents, behavior, and consequences. An example of this pro-cess is the following description about the hypothetical student Mary who hit her classmate five times on his head during the read-ing period. The antecedent is thought to be that when Mary is given written questions about the chapter she is reading, they appear too difficult for her because she asks Billy for help, which he refuses. Each time that he refuses, she hits him on the head with her fist (five times total). He finally turns around after the fifth time and lets her see his answers. The purpose for the behavior appears to be that Mary needs help and wants Billy to assist her.

The fourth step in the development of the ISP would be to change the antecedents by making the questions easier and more developmentally appropriate for Mary. The fifth step of the ISP is to substitute a more positive behavior, which can be accomplished by teaching her to raise her hand when she needs assistance and then the teacher will help her. The consequences are then changed be-cause Mary receives praise for performing the desired behavior in-stead of getting into trouble for hurting her classmate. Another pos-itive consequence would be for the teacher to ask Billy to be her peer tutor. If he agrees, a more friendly relationship between the two students could develop, and this would be considered a second positive consequence.

In order for the alternative behavior to be effective, it should be as easy or easier to perform than the original, negative behavior (O'Neill, 1997). The student needs to be taught how and when to ef-fectively use the new skill. Then the adult must pay positive atten-tion to the student for demonstrating the desired behavior. The skill then can be generalized to different environments and in natural sit-uations when needed, such as during the math period when Mary requires assistance in answering story problems. The ISP is espe-cially effective in helping children with behavior difficulties who are maltreated because it can improve their behaviors within sup-portive, caring relationships with teachers and peers. It also benefits the children because they learn what to do to improve as well as what not to do.

OTHER BEHAVIOR MANAGEMENT TECHNIQUES

Other techniques for behavior management can sometimes be implemented to assist students who are at risk. These techniques include contingency contracting, token economies, and shaping. Contingency contracting is based on the Premack Principle (Premack, 1959), which states that a behavior that occurs often can be used to increase one that happens less frequently. This principle is often referred to as "Grandma's law." An example of the Premack Principle is, "If you eat your vegetables, you can have dessert." Contingency contracting consists of a written or verbal contract between the student and the teacher. The student agrees to correct the misbehavior, and the teacher gives the student something he or she wants in return. The contract is developed by both parties and signed. It specifies the exact behavior to be changed, a time limit for the change, and a reward for changing it (Lerner, 2000).

A token economy is another behavior management technique, which consists of reinforcers that are combined and exchanged for a more meaningful one. Examples of tokens are poker chips or toy cars that are collected by the students and later exchanged for desired activities (e.g., longer recess, computer time) or for tangible reinforcers (e.g., toys, games, food) (Lerner, 2000; Walker & Shea, 1999).

Shaping is a behavior technique that involves breaking down a desired behavioral goal into a sequence of attainable steps and then reinforcing the child for performing each step until the goal is reached. A hypothetical example of a goal would be for Walter, who is hyperactive, to be able to sit in his seat for 5 minutes. First, Walter is reinforced for sitting 1 minute, then 2, then 3, then 4, and then finally 5 minutes when the goal is attained. All of these behavior management techniques can help children who are at risk for maltreatment with disruptive behaviors to improve and act more appropriately.

SOCIAL SKILLS TRAINING

This section of the chapter discusses methods of teaching social skills that are difficult for some children who are maltreated to acquire because of the lack of adequate modeling by their caregivers who are abusive or neglectful. The following are the social skills that frequently need to be taught (Bos &Vaughn, 1998; Walker & Shea, 1999):

- Appropriate body language (e.g., appropriate gestures, eye contact, and facial expressions)
- Alternative behaviors to aggression (e.g., asking permission, sharing, negotiating, keeping self-control, refraining from fighting)
- Appropriate greetings, including the selection of appropriate ways to greet people and ways to respond to their greetings
- Coping with stress (e.g., how to react when not accepted, respond to failure, cope with embarrassment, and react to group pressure)
- Initiating and maintaining communication with others (e.g., ways to initiate conversations, compliment others, ask appropriate questions, and respond to both positive and negative feedback)

General Instruction of Social Skills

There are a variety of ways to teach social skills, which consist of individual and group instruction, games and role playing, and instruction in personal problem solving (Lerner, 2000). Teaching methods generally involve modeling, rehearsing the skill, and transferring or generalizing it to other relevant, natural environments. Instruction usually is done in a sequence of stages (Elksnin & Elksnin, 1998). The first stage is to identify the needed skill and then clearly define it for the student. The second stage is to provide the reasons for learning the skill. It is important for the student to understand the benefits of acquiring the skill so that he or she is motivated to learn it (e.g., "If I ask Billy for a turn instead of grabbing his truck, we can play together, and I won't get in trouble with my teacher"). In the third stage of instruction, the teacher and student brainstorm ideas about how the skill can be helpful in diverse situations and with different people. The fourth stage is role-playing or acting out these situations using the target social skill. In role playing, the teacher first models the skill, next guides the student to imitate it, and then provides opportunities for the student to practice it independently. The teacher can give positive feedback, in the form of praise, for effort and success. Peers also can assist in both role-playing and providing this feedback. The last stage of the training consists of helping the student generalize the skill to other natural environments (Bos & Vaughn, 1998). Practicing the skill until mastery is achieved also fosters generalization.

Additional Methods of Training Social Skills

Other methods of training social skills involve the use of mnemonic strategies, such as FAST and SLAM (Vaughn et al., 2000; Vaughn &

LaGreca, 1993). The purpose of the FAST strategy is to assist children in their interpersonal problem solving. It consists of four steps. The following is a summary:

F   *Freeze and think.* What is the problem I have getting along with this person?

A   *Alternatives.* What solutions can I think of to try?

S   *Solution.* Which one seems to be the best and most fair to both of us?

T   *Try it.* I'll try it, and if it does not work, I'll think of others.

The SLAM strategy also uses mnemonics. The purpose of SLAM is to assist students in accepting negative feedback in a constructive way. The four steps in SLAM are the following:

S   *Stop.* Children are taught to stop what they are doing, take a deep breath, and listen to the person who is giving them negative feedback.

L   *Look.* The students are told to establish eye contact and look directly at the person instead of looking down or away.

A   *Ask.* The children are told to ask questions in order to clearly understand the reasons for the negative feedback.

M   *Make.* The children are taught to make a response that can consist of agreeing with the feedback, stopping the behavior that caused the feedback, or clearly explaining the other person's perspective of the situation.

Both the SLAM and the FAST strategies often need a great deal of practice until the students have mastered them and are successful in their use.

TRAINING IN SELECTED SOCIAL SKILLS

Certain social skills have been selected for specific instruction because of their importance to many children who are maltreated in their interpersonal relationships. These skills are making friends, constructively recognizing and expressing emotions, controlling anger, managing conflict, developing a sense of internal control, and building self-esteem.

Making Friends

Children who are maltreated often feel isolated from their peers. These children have difficulty making and keeping friends. Instruction in this skill can begin with a class discussion on the meaning and value of friendships (Salend, 1999). The teacher can then focus the instruction on how to give emotional support to friends, how to respond to friendly overtures, how to join a playgroup, and how to maintain friendships as well as have the students practice positive social interactions. Class activities that assist the development of friendships include group art projects, sing-along groups, friendship posters, class newspapers and bulletin boards, journals about the value of friendship, cooperative games, and books and videos that depict friendliness and acceptance (Salend, 1999). A class buddy system is another aide in making friends. In this system, a peer who is more popular is paired with a child who is less popular to play games or make projects. The higher social status of the peer tends to make the child who is less popular more socially acceptable to the rest of the students, and they are encouraged to play with the child who is less popular. The class buddy and the peer who is less popular might even develop a good friendship through their work together.

Recognizing and Expressing Emotions

Classrooms that are emotionally safe encourage children to acknowledge their emotions and constructively express them. Children who are maltreated, who may have to hide their negative emotions at home because of the threats of caregivers who are abusive, are free in these classrooms to express their feelings, whether they are negative or positive. These children are not criticized or punished when they do this. For example, if they are angry with the teacher or with a peer, they can say how they feel instead of acting out their feelings with aggression. Teachers can help their students recognize their emotions by mirroring them and talking about them. The display of feelings by the children is considered a form of nonverbal communication that is important for their emotional development (Beaty, 1999). Children who are maltreated need their feelings understood and valued before they can recognize and value those of others. Teachers should be aware of and recognize when their students appear happy, angry, sad, upset, and so forth, and then discuss the reasons with them. In addition, children who are maltreated need to see their teachers display their genuine emotions so they can learn from this modeling. If the teachers feel happy, their facial expressions and gestures should show it. In contrast, if they are angry, they should demonstrate this feeling as well through their body language. Other activities that help children recognize and describe their emotions are learning more vocabulary that describes feelings, identifying and describing pictures of different people displaying a range of emotions, drawing faces and interpreting feelings from their facial expressions, reading stories that describe people's emotions, and playing games in which the children make faces at each other and guess which feelings they are projecting.

Controlling Anger

Controlling one's anger is another area in which a number of children who are maltreated need assistance; many of these children are full of rage as a result of being abused. Snell and Janney (2000) proposed training children to control anger through successive steps. The first step is assisting the students in identifying the events that lead up to the anger or recognizing what triggers it. Once the children can identify the triggers, they can take steps to control their anger. The triggers could be within themselves (e.g., feeling that other children are always picking on them) or they could be outside events (e.g., not being accepted on a sports team). The second step is assisting the students in recognizing physical symptoms of anger, such as clenched fists, frowns, or tight muscles. The last step is teaching anger reducers, such as counting to 10; deep breathing; remembering pleasant events; and foreseeing the negative consequences of uncontrolled anger, which could lead to aggression and trouble with peers and adults.

Managing Conflict

Managing conflict also can be problematic for many children who are abused and neglected because of the lack of adequate modeling of this skill by their caregivers. Conflict management should be repeatedly practiced or overlearned because of its importance in interpersonal relationships. Johnson and Johnson (1996) explained that when negotiating agreements in conflicts, the children have to define and describe their disagreement and then look at their own perspectives of the problem, consider those of the other individuals involved in the conflicts, brainstorm with them some agreeable solutions to both parties, and then choose one together to implement. A constructive solution to a conflict is one that produces joint benefits, is workable, is cooperative, and encourages consideration of other alternatives if the solution is unsuccessful (Johnson & Johnson, 1995).

Another method of conflict management, which has shown success in some studies, is the use of peer mediators who are responsible for negotiating constructive solutions when their classmates have conflicts (Johnson & Johnson, 1998). Peer mediation can be taught to all students in the following sequence:

1. End the hostility or break up the fight.
2. Allow the students involved to calm down and cool their tempers.
3. Obtain their commitments to the mediation process.
4. Use the steps previously described in conflict management.
5. Draw up a contract when an agreement is reached.

After the conflict, the peer mediators then monitor to make sure the contract is followed.

Developing a Sense of Internal Control

Establishing a sense of internal or inner control is also beneficial for children who are maltreated because many of them may have defeatist attitudes in their interpersonal relationships with other children and adults. Because of their lack of control over what happens to them at home, they believe that they also will be unsuccessful at controlling their interactions at school. Their belief is that no matter what they do, they will not have positive relationships with others. If they happen to be lucky and make a friend, for example, they attribute this to external reasons, such as luck or circumstance, and not to their own efforts. They have acquired an external locus of control. Teachers can help these children develop an internal sense of control by pointing out the cause and effect of their behaviors and emphasizing the association between how they interact and how others respond. Role playing and successful practicing in natural situations will assist them in realizing they can be in control, are responsible for their interpersonal relationships, and can make these relationships positive by their own efforts (Lerner, 2000; Stipek, 1993).

Building Self-Esteem

Self-esteem was described by Putnam (1998) as a feeling people have about whether they are worthy individuals. Self-esteem is related to people's self-concepts, which define who they are, what they can do now, and what they are capable of doing in the future (Beaty, 1999). This self-judgment depends a great deal on how competent, accepted, and well-liked a person thinks he or she is. Individuals with positive self-concepts believe they are appreciated and respected by others. This may not be the case for some children who are abused, however, because of the continual negative feedback they receive about themselves from their caregivers. This type of negative response undermines their self-esteem and feelings of worthiness (Haager & Vaughn, 1995).

Teachers can assist these children in gaining self-esteem and self-confidence through a variety of strategies consisting of offering these children many experiences in which they are cared for and loved unconditionally regardless of their behaviors. Although teachers may not like certain behaviors, they should always accept the children as being worthy. Discovering and acknowledging their talents will build self-esteem. One role of the teacher is to discover the students' expertise and make sure that the other children and adults at school are aware of and give positive reinforcement (e.g., praise) for their abilities. Another method of fostering self-esteem is to have a "fail-safe" classroom in which errors are regarded as ways of learning rather than criticized. The more competent children feel, the better their self-worth will be. Positive school experiences (e.g., helping younger, less mature children by being tutors or buddies; being given responsibilities) can build self-confidence in children who are maltreated. Positions of responsibility may include line leader, paper passer, teacher helper, calendar person, pet feeder, and so forth, as well as volunteering in service projects. Participation in extracurricular activities also should be encouraged because it fosters a sense of acceptance and belonging and also offers a haven for children who are at risk from possible maltreatment at home. Some extracurricular activities include school clubs, hobby groups, sports, arts and crafts, school choirs, orchestras, and plays.

THE EDUCATOR'S ROLE IN FACILITATING RESILIENCY

Because of their continual availability, teachers can facilitate resiliency in children who are maltreated. These children, who may lack attachment models in their families, can develop trust and warm relationships with their teachers who act as surrogate caregivers. Resiliency is enhanced when children are cared about and respected. Teachers who serve as models of resiliency have the greatest effect on children who are at risk when they provide them with a caring, respectful class environment with appropriate structure and limits (Brooks, 1994; Brooks & Rice, 1997). According to Lopez (1999), teachers foster resiliency when they stress a number of basic values beginning with the letter A, as can be seen in the following summary:

A   *Approval.* Teachers should be sure to recognize what children achieve, no matter how little, and let them know that they approve of them.

A   *Acceptance.* Teachers should make certain that their students realize that they accept them unconditionally, regardless of how they behave.

A   *Attention.* Teachers should give positive attention to each child.

A   *Appreciation.* Teachers should appreciate the efforts of the students as well as their achievements.

A   *Affection.* Teachers should show their regard for students by welcoming each one as an important member of the classroom community. They should smile often and use a warm tone of voice whenever possible.

CONCLUSION

This chapter has examined strategies and social-emotional interventions that teachers can implement to make their classrooms nurturing and safe for children who are maltreated. The next chapter focuses on methods of teaching academic subjects that can provide children who are maltreated with success.

8

EFFECTIVE
TEACHING STRATEGIES

This chapter describes methods of teaching and instructional strategies to assist children who are maltreated in learning in the classroom and achieving academic success. Because of the possible negative effects on the development of verbal–linguistic and mathematical skills, previously mentioned in Chapter 3, some children who are maltreated have difficulty succeeding in language and math classes, which are valued in many schools. If given opportunities, however, they can demonstrate their strengths in other ways. Teachers can help these children through the use of a variety of teaching strategies that match their different abilities (Kagan, 1998). Their individual strengths then can be used to assist them in overcoming their weaknesses and improving their self-confidence in mastering academic tasks.

The first teaching strategy discussed is cooperative learning, in which students work together to solve problems and find solutions to academic tasks. As indicated by a review of research by Slavin (1995), important outcomes of cooperative learning for children who are maltreated can include raising academic self-esteem, providing multiple experiences for active learning, and helping students practice effective social skills. The second teaching strategy described is peer tutoring, which is described as a beneficial supplement to cooperative learning. In peer tutoring, students that are in the same class take turns helping one another. The third instructional technique discussed is derived from *Multiple Intelligences: The Theory in Practice,* by Gardner (1993), who hypothesizes that intelligence is not just one entity but rather it is composed of multiple ones. If instruction is compatible with the unique intelligences of children who are maltreated, then success in academics is facilitated. Following this discussion, scaffolding and reciprocal teaching are discussed, which have developed from a cognitive theory. The basis for these strategies is the *theory of social influences on learning* (Vygotsky, 1962), which states that teacher mediation and interactions with students facilitate their learning. Other techniques are then described to improve the cognitive skills of organization, attention, and memory; to make adaptations of the school environment; and to modify the curriculum. The last section of this chapter discusses special instruction in language and mathematics, which will assist children who are maltreated to become more successful in these areas (Burl, 1992; Kurtz, Gaudin, Wodarski, & Howing, 1993; Radford, 1998). It is important to remember, however, that the most important ingredient of effectively teaching students who are abused or neglected is providing plentiful guidance, encouragement, and support for their efforts and achievements. This final chapter concludes with the reiteration of the fervent hope and vision that teachers can make a positive difference in the lives of children who are maltreated.

COOPERATIVE LEARNING

Cooperative learning methods have been defined by Slavin as "instructional techniques in which students work in heterogeneous learning teams to help one another learn academic material" (1991, p. 177). A number of features of cooperative learning can benefit children who are maltreated, including 1) its emphasis on success for all children, 2) its recognition of each student's achievements, and 3) its modeling and practice of useful social skills. The first two features build academic self-esteem and confidence, which are so essential to the successful educational performance of children who are maltreated. The third feature assists these children in gaining the acceptance of their peers.

Cooperative learning stresses the positive interdependence of students instead of having them compete with each other for school achievement. This negative interdependence forces students to attain success at the expense of their peers. In positive interdependence, the students work together to ensure that each one is successful. Thus, academic success comes from the cooperation of each learner in the group and is not based on competition (Johnson & Johnson, 1996). Cooperative learning also encourages constructive face-to-face interaction among all of the students on a team.

The teammates share thoughts and experiences and recognize each other's accomplishments.

Another feature of cooperative learning is the accountability of each team member who has the responsibility to help complete the assignment and demonstrate progress. Each student, however, can fulfill this objective by the use of his or her preferred learning style, which fosters success and achievement. Methods of accountability include constructive self-evaluation, team assessment, and teacher evaluations. Social skills for work and play (e.g., effective communication, problem solving, recognition of others' ideas, conflict management, respect for others, the ability to compromise) also are practiced in cooperative learning. These skills need to be taught by the teacher, modeled and practiced by the children, and monitored for effective use. The last step in the process of cooperative learning is for the students and the teachers to evaluate whether the cooperative learning has been successful. Constructive feedback is essential from all involved for making future improvements and can shown students who are mistreated that their contributions are respected and valued (Abruscato, 1994; Orlich, Harder, Callahan, & Gibson, 1998). All of these characteristics and features of cooperative learning are identified by Kagan (1995) in the acronym PIES, which stands for the following four principles:

P   Positive interdependence or "all for one, one for all"—Everyone in the learning group contributes to its success.

I   Individual accountability—There is individual accountability as well as group accountability.

E   Equal participation—Each one contributes and participates equally.

S   Simultaneous interactions—There can be a number of positive interactions within the group occurring at the same time.

Kagan (1998) has incorporated these principles into an instructional plan called "Timed-Pair-Share" in which the students work in pairs. One of the pair is labeled A, and the other B. First, all of the As in the pairs share their ideas about their assignments, and the Bs listen for 1 minute. Then, the opposite occurs in which the Bs relate their thoughts, and the As listen for 1 minute. This procedure ensures equal participation of each partner in each pair. Individual accountability also is provided because both members of each pair are individually accountable for their efforts and work. Positive interdependence is demonstrated because each partner needs to understand the ideas of the other one in the pair. Cooperative learning then can result in more learning because of the active participation of both partners.

Types of Cooperative Learning and Implementation

Teachers can implement cooperative learning for different purposes. These purposes include teaching specific content, helping the students further understand the content through discussion and practice, and providing the necessary support for mastery (Johnson & Johnson, 1998). Any academic task can be accomplished by cooperative learning. For example, students can work together completing experiments in science, making social studies reports, and practicing ways to solve story problems in mathematics. Cooperative learning, however, takes a great deal of planning by teachers to ensure its success. First, groups need to be formed that take into account many factors, such as learning styles, ability levels, temperaments, and interests. Learning groups usually have members of varying abilities who support one another to achieve the group goals. Sometimes, teachers can match children according to a shared interest, such as art, music, or history. The groups may be time limited and last from 1 week to a whole semester depending on the nature of the assignments and the students' abilities to work together. According to some studies (Orlich et al., 1998), the most beneficial time limits are 3–9 weeks, after which the groups should be changed to enable students to learn to interact and work with different classmates.

Roles may be assigned to the group members, or they can just arise naturally. Roles include but are not limited to the group leader, who is responsible for overseeing that everyone on the team is working on the goals; the group manager, who makes sure that everyone has the appropriate materials; the team monitor, who ensures that each group member is on task; the group reporter, who arranges the reporting of the activities by the team to the rest of the class; and the group recorder, who records the accomplishments of the team (Johnson & Johnson, 1995).

When implementing cooperative learning, teachers often follow a general instructional sequence. First, the teacher needs to specify the learning goals for each group by explaining each one to be achieved. Then, necessary learning strategies are taught, and the concepts of interdependence and individual accountability are discussed with the group members. The next task is for the teacher to monitor whether the groups are meeting their goals and to intervene if there are difficulties. Finally, the teacher and the members of the team evaluate their success. If they have not been successful, then everyone is consulted about improvements. Cooperative learning is valuable for all students because of its versatility in meeting everyone's needs (Johnson & Johnson, 1998).

PEER TUTORING

Cooperative learning is sometimes combined with another instructional technique known as peer tutoring, which benefits children who are maltreated because it provides individualized practice in learning the concepts and mastering the learning objectives. Thus, this technique builds these students' knowledge and self-confidence in academic tasks. In peer tutoring, two students work together on a learning task. One child takes the role of the tutor, while the other one is the tutee (Lerner, 2000). Other advantages of peer tutoring for students who are maltreated are that it provides more time to review difficult school assignments, the tutees can get immediate feedback from the tutors about the accuracy of their responses, and social skills can be fostered through the interactions of the students (Greenwood, 1996). The tutors also can perfect their learning, because the best way to really learn a subject often is to teach it to someone else. Peer tutoring usually is implemented by students of the same age. This instructional technique, however, can be used with children of different ages and developmental levels in which case it is referred to as cross-age tutoring.

In both types of tutoring, training is necessary for the tutors to be successful. The training consists of the following steps: 1) The teacher demonstrates how to tutor a particular tutee; 2) then, the tutor models the demonstration and practices it with teacher guidance; 3) next, other students role-play the part of the tutee while the tutor practices; and 4) finally, the peer tutor has an actual session with the tutee with teacher assistance and reinforcement. Following this, other tutoring sessions are scheduled with occasional teacher observations and feedback until the learning goals are achieved (Snell & Brown, 2000).

Specific programs of peer tutoring have been investigated. One successful program is Reciprocal Peer Tutoring (Greenwood, 1996) in which the tutor–tutee partners work together on teams. Reciprocal Peer Tutoring requires that the partners alternate the roles of tutors and tutees to eliminate any possible feelings of superiority of the tutors to the tutees. This exchange provides children who are maltreated and who are academically at risk with opportunities to tutor peers who are not maltreated, which can increase their self-esteem and acceptance by their classmates. More positive social relationships then can be facilitated. The general instructional sequence of Reciprocal Peer Tutoring is first, the materials are prepared for the lesson; second, the lesson is introduced; third, the tutors and tutees are chosen and assigned to teams; fourth, the roles are exchanged between the tutors and tutees after specific time periods; and finally, the teams earn points contingent on their successful performances (Utley, Mortsweet, & Greenwood, 1997).

The research on peer tutoring programs in general has indicated its success (Fisher, Schumaker, & Deshler, 1995; Fuchs & Fuchs, 1998; Greenwood & Terry, 1997). Important advantages of these programs are thought to be that children enjoy them; they are not difficult to initiate, implement, and maintain; and that improvements in both academic abilities and social skills have been noted (Harper, Mallette, & Moore, 1991; Utley et al., 1997). For students who are maltreated, an important benefit would be the ability of peer tutoring programs to accommodate their individualized strengths and needs (Franca, Kerr, Reitz, & Lambert, 1990; Fuchs & Fuchs, 1998; Fuchs, Fuchs, & Burish, 2000; Garcia, 1992).

INSTRUCTION TECHNIQUES DERIVED FROM THEORIES

This section examines some teaching strategies that are derived from two theories: the *theory of multiple intelligences* (Gardner, 1993) and the *theory of social influences on learning* (Vygotsky, 1978). Both of these theories have important educational implications for instructing students who are maltreated.

Theory of Multiple Intelligences

As mentioned previously, the *theory of multiple intelligences* (MI) suggests that there are many types of intelligences, not just one (Gardner, 1993). This theory benefits children who are maltreated because of its hypothesis that their unique types of intelligences can be used to assist them in being successful in school. Specific types of intelligences mentioned in this theory are the following:

- Verbal-linguistic emphasizes verbal skills, such as oral and written language.
- Logical-mathematical stresses problem solving, logic, and mathematical reasoning.
- Visual-spatial focuses on directional, artistic, and architectural abilities.
- Musical-rhythmic emphasizes musical talents, such as singing, composing, appreciating, and performing in music.
- Bodily-kinesthetic stresses movement, such as in dance or sports.
- Naturalistic focuses on animal husbandry, the ability to grow plants and flowers, and the appreciation of nature.

- Interpersonal emphasizes talents in leadership, teaming, and social skills.
- Intrapersonal stresses accurate knowledge of one's self, self-direction, and control.

MI instruction matches teaching strategies with the types of intelligences that are relatively strong in each child. Therefore, this kind of teaching is responsive to the individual child's learning style. For example, if given an event in history to remember, a child who is musically talented could compose a song about it, a budding artist could remember the event by drawing a picture of it, and a child who has good social skills could report on the social interactions that occurred during the event to refresh his or her memory of it. Thus, students who are maltreated, who may have different learning styles, can be recognized and valued for their contributions (Gardner, 1993).

This favorable recognition is of utmost importance in building their self-esteem and pride in their schoolwork. MI theory also suggests that teachers can better develop the cognitive abilities of their students by including each type of intelligence in the curriculum. Then, by just modifying the curriculum, learning is facilitated for students who are maltreated and who are at risk for academic problems.

Theory of Social Influences on Learning

The *theory of social influences on learning* stresses the social nature of intellectual development and the important role of interpersonal relationships in learning (Vygotsky, 1978). In applying this theory to children who are maltreated and have learning difficulties, these children may be able, with teacher mediation, to successfully master tasks originally thought to be too difficult for them (Smith-Trawick, 2000). This can improve their self-confidence and elevate their social status when peers recognize their achievements. The author of the theory, Lev Vygotsky, hypothesized that teachers and caregivers use language and social interactions to guide a child's thought process. Vygotsky referred to this guidance as "scaffolding." When children can do a task independently, the teachers do not interfere. When the task is somewhat challenging, however, the teachers ask questions or give prompts to help the children problem-solve ways to master the assignment. Through this verbal mediation, the students are encouraged to demonstrate more of their actual potentials. Vygotsky (1978) named this process the *zone of proximal development.*

In addition to scaffolding, another teaching technique called reciprocal teaching has been developed from this theory (Palincsar & Klenk, 1992). The premise of reciprocal teaching is that children learn best through a social dialogue with their teachers. In this dialogue, teachers and students take turns in leading discussions about shared texts and learning materials (Vaughn, Bos, & Schumm, 2000). Active learning and comprehension are emphasized in this approach (Bos & Vaughn, 1998). Reciprocal teaching consists of the following four activities (Lerner, 2000):

1. The text is read silently by the students and the teacher.
2. Then, the teacher describes and models aloud the techniques of questioning, clarifying, summarizing, and predicting, all of which assist the students in comprehending the text.
3. Next, some of the students are chosen to read another section of the text and model the teacher's techniques to the other classmates. The role of the teacher is to guide and prompt the students if they have difficulties. This process is similar to that of scaffolding, which was previously discussed.
4. The final activity is for the students to practice and master these techniques, which assist them in understanding the subject matter.

Reciprocal teaching can be valuable for students who are maltreated because of its fail-safe nature that builds self-confidence in learning. Errors are not criticized, and the children are gently guided to comprehend text that otherwise might be too difficult for them. In addition, they are actively involved in their learning and have opportunities to demonstrate their abilities and receive recognition through the praise of both their teachers and peers. These positive reinforcements can further the self-esteem and confidence of children who are maltreated and encourage their participation in challenging academic work.

OTHER INSTRUCTIONAL
TECHNIQUES FOR IMPROVING COGNITIVE SKILLS

Children who are maltreated may need assistance in developing other cognitive skills, which may not be modeled by their caregivers but are very necessary for school and other daily living activities. These skills include organization, attention to the task, and memory.

Improving Organizational Skills

Tips for teachers on how to improve the organizational abilities of their students are provided by Lerner, Lowenthal, and Lerner (1995). The following is a modified summary:

- Designate a specific place for the students to keep their materials and possessions at school.
- Help the students plan ahead by scheduling specific blocks of time to finish their assignments. Give each child a copy of the schedule.
- Provide the students with different colored notebooks for each assignment.
- Give the students a list of materials needed for each task.
- Tape-record information about due dates for assignments so that students can review them if necessary.
- Avoid multiple assignments. Give the students just one at a time.
- Ask the students to wear backpacks to carry their homework and materials.

Improving Attention Span and Ability to Focus

Students who are maltreated may initially pay attention to an academic task but become easily distracted within a short period of time. The following are some methods to lengthen these students' attention spans (Turnbull, Turnbull, Shank, & Leal, 1999):

- Shorten the students' assignments (e.g., decrease the number of spelling words they need to learn).
- Increase the novelty of the task so that the students become more interested in doing it.
- When repetition is necessary, alternate rote practice with relevant games to rehearse the material.
- Underline important information so that the students attend to it.
- Follow less interesting assignments with more interesting ones.
- Alternate written and oral instructions.
- Allow extra time for these students to complete work.
- When necessary, provide peer assistance for these students to take notes.

Improving Memory Skills

Sometimes children who are maltreated, because of their difficulties in attending, also may have problems in memorizing information necessary for tests and assignments. There are a number of instructional strategies that may aid these students' memory skills (Bos & Vaughn, 1998). First, it is important that teachers stress the new concepts to be learned at the beginning of the lesson. Second, teachers should assist the students in connecting the new information with any previous knowledge of the subject. Third, visual aides (e.g., pictures, charts, overheads) can be used to make the information easier to remember. Fourth, teachers should provide time for these students to practice and review the new concepts. The fifth and last recommendation is for the teachers to assist the students in learning mnemonic strategies, which simplify the information to be recalled. Mnemonic strategies stress the process of association, categorization, visualization, and verbal repetition to assist memory. An example of association is the use of acronyms (e.g., the first letters of the words to remember), such as in the SLAM or FAST strategies described in Chapter 6. An example of categorization is dividing the information into categories (e.g., plants, animals), which makes it easier to remember. The process of visualization requires seeing in the mind's eye a picture of what needs to be recalled. Verbal repetition assists memory through oral rehearsal of the information (Hughes, 1996; Lerner, 2000).

MODIFICATIONS AND ADAPTATIONS

Students who are maltreated may need special modifications and/ or adaptations to assist their learning and increase their mastery of schoolwork. These modifications and adaptations may include adapting the environment and modifying the objectives of the curriculum, the responses required, the presentation, the workload, and the materials. An alternate type of modification is the use of task analysis.

Adapting the School Environment

The school environment influences the teaching and learning processes. Teachers can use the following adaptations to make the school environment more positive for students who are maltreated (Nevin, 1998; Yehle & Rambold, 1998):

- The teacher should reduce unnecessary clutter to make the classroom more attractive.
- The students should sit in close proximity to the teacher. The proximity often has the effect of lengthening the students' attention span.

- The students' seats should be away from high traffic areas, which can distract them.
- The teacher should have all necessary equipment in order and materials prepared ahead of time to reduce possible distractibility from waiting time.
- The teacher should examine the schedule to reduce waiting times.
- The teacher should divide the classroom into small groups to increase the students' attention while teaching lessons. If possible, the teacher should reduce class size through the use of aides and volunteers.
- The teacher should define each student's workspace during large-group floor activities (e.g., providing each child with a carpet square on which to sit).
- If the teacher has a student who is hyperactive in his or her class, then the student should be allowed to stand while doing seatwork, especially at the end of the task.
- The students should be given two seats in which to move around when necessary.
- The teacher should cover the students' desks with colored contact paper to attract their attention to the schoolwork.

Modifying the Objective, Response, Workload, and Materials

To meet the needs of students who are maltreated who have learning difficulties, modifications may be necessary in the objective of the lesson, presentation of it, response, workload, and material. The following modifications are summarized from the recommendations of Lerner (2000), Snell and Janney (2000), and Yehle and Rambold (1998):

1. Same objective with an alternate response (e.g., all of the students work on the same objective, but instead of writing the answers down on an assignment, a student is allowed to give the answers orally)
2. Same objective but with an alternate presentation (e.g., when a student has difficulties in reading, a peer can read him or her the assigned chapters)
3. Same objective but less of a workload (e.g., instead of assigning 10 math problems, 5 are given to the student)
4. Same objective with different materials and expectations (e.g., instead of learning seventh-grade spelling words, the student learns second-grade level words so that the objective is similar but fulfilled at a lower level of development)

5. Individualized objective (e.g., instead of doing story problems in mathematics, the student works on coin and dollar recognition and the counting of change as a way to make the objective more functional and relate to life skills)

When planning modifications, teachers need to keep in mind the significant components of the curriculum so that all of these components will be included in the changes. Modifications should be meaningful, useful, and meet the individual needs of children who are maltreated so that they are actively involved, work with their peers, participate fully in class activities, and achieve success. It also is important for teachers to be culturally sensitive to diversity in students who are abused and neglected so that their expectations do not conflict with their students' cultural backgrounds. For example, teachers should not expect eye contact from all of their students when they answer questions if this would be a sign of disrespect to adults in some children's cultures.

Using Task Analysis as an Alternate Modification

Another type of modification involves the use of task analysis, which can facilitate learning in some students who are abused and neglected. The purpose of task analysis is to break down a task into small, manageable, and sequential units (Lerner, 2000). Instead of being overwhelmed by a task, the student can feel more confident of its mastery. In planning the task analysis, the teacher should decide on the important information that must be learned, the sequence of steps in teaching it, and the necessary prerequisite skills. This information can be obtained by answering the following questions:

*   Is the task verbal or nonverbal? Is it auditory or visual?
*   What problem-solving strategies are necessary for the mastery of each step?
*   How will the student demonstrate mastery of the whole assignment?

Task analysis can assist students who are maltreated by reducing the complexity of an assignment so that they feel successful and gain a sense of mastery.

STRATEGIES FOR ORAL LANGUAGE DEVELOPMENT

Some studies have indicated that a number of young children who are abused and neglected have delays in their development of oral language (Culp, Little, Letts, & Lawrence, 1991; Ekenrode, Laird, &

Doris, 1993; Radford, 1998). The reasons for their language difficulties are thought to be a lack of verbal stimulation by neglectful caregivers and frequent experiences of being criticized or punished by abusive caregivers that decrease the children's motivation to talk about their activities, label objects, and ask questions. In addition, adults who abuse their children may offer few opportunities for the children to provide verbal feedback. Consequently, these children may withdraw and talk very little or instead act out their feelings in nonverbal ways through physical aggression. Thus, they do not develop effective receptive and expressive language skills.

Some studies have also indicated that children who are maltreated have particular problems in the pragmatics of language or the use of language in social situations and the verbal expression of their emotions (Kurtz et al., 1993; Radford, 1998). There are a number of interventions that classroom teachers, in collaboration with speech and language therapists, can implement to assist these students in their language skills. The following strategies are described in this section: naturalistic teaching, milieu teaching, responsive interaction, self-talk, classroom interventions for improvement of pragmatics, activity-based intervention, peer-mediated intervention, and techniques to improve listening skills.

Naturalistic Teaching

Naturalistic teaching is language instruction that takes place in daily routines and activities in the classroom instead of in isolated therapy rooms. Other characteristics of naturalistic teaching are that the topics of conversation are child-initiated and follow the child's interests. The continuation of the child-initiated activity and the topic of interest are the natural reinforcements for communication. Teaching strategies focus on modeling developmentally appropriate language, balancing the length and frequency of turn taking by the child and adult in communicative exchanges, responding to the child's efforts to communicate, and incidental prompting to obtain more complex language (Yoder et al., 1995). Two examples of naturalistic language interventions are milieu teaching and responsive interaction.

Milieu Teaching

Milieu teaching is a strategy in which teachers or other adults deliberately arrange the environment to encourage a child's language (Kaiser & Hester, 1994). The adult follows the child's interest and teaches language by providing specific prompts, corrections, and reinforcements for child responses. The language training also occurs in natural environments, routines, and activities. Three procedures in milieu teaching are the following:

1. The first procedure is the mand-model procedure in which the teacher attends to the child's choice of an activity or toy, requests or mands a response from the child about the activity, provides a model to imitate, and then gives the child the toy or material of interest.

2. The second procedure is the use of a time delay in which the teacher looks at the child expectantly or questioningly for 15 seconds. The delay gives the child time to respond before the adult provides a model of the appropriate language. The adult may repeat the model twice, each time waiting for the child to talk before giving the child what he or she wants.

3. The third procedure is incidental teaching. This procedure requires that the child initiates a topic of conversation and that the adult converses about the topic. The teacher follows the child's lead and only stays with the topic as long as the child is attentive. If the adult focuses on the same topic as the child, joint attention of both participants is assured. By talking in short, simple sentences and by repeating often, teachers can stimulate the language development of students who are at risk during daily routines. This type of intervention is thought to generalize more efficiently than direct teaching of language because the language training resembles natural language interactions. Milieu teaching also has been demonstrated to be more effective than direct teaching for children in the early stages of language development (Yoder et al., 1995).

Responsive Interaction

The intervention of responsive interaction does not use prompts as in milieu teaching. Instead, responsive interaction places emphasis on developing an interaction style that promotes balanced turn taking and communication between the teacher and the child (Mahoney & Neville-Smith, 1996). This intervention is based on the theory that children learn new language and will use their existing language more often when they hear appropriate language models in their interactions with responsive adults. Teachers learn the basic principles of responsive interactions, such as following the child's lead, taking turns, matching and extending the child's topic of conversation, and providing developmentally appropriate language models. Teaching strategies include the use of expansions, expatiations, parallel talk, and self-talk. These techniques are appropriate for young children who are maltreated who are acquiring language and for older students who developmentally are at the same stage.

Expansion Expansion is useful for children who are talking but who are not talking in complete sentences. The teacher listens to the child's words, tries to understand the whole idea that the child wants to communicate, and repeats the sentence in a more complete, but simple, form. The teacher lets the child know that he or she was understood and presents the child with a more complete language model (Donahue-Kilburg, 1992). The following conversation illustrates expansion:

> Child: "Go." (points to the door)
> Teacher: "Go out?"
> Child: "Go out." (shakes head to indicate yes)
> Teacher: "You want to go out now?"
> Child: "Go."
> Teacher: "Go out now."
> Child: "Go out now."

Expatiation Expatiation is accomplished by first following the child's lead in conversation. The teacher focuses on what the child says, not on the way it is said. The teacher lets the child know that he or she has listened and then adds new information. The following illustrates expatiation:

> Child: "Boy eats."
> Teacher: "Yes, he's eating crackers."

Parallel Talk Parallel talk is the strategy of describing what the child is doing or seeing. For example, if a young child is banging a block on the classroom floor, the teacher may say the following: "Hit the block. Hit the block on the floor. Bang, bang, bang. Hit the block."

Self-Talk

When using the strategy of self-talk, adults talk about what they are doing, seeing, or feeling as the youngster listens nearby. For example, if a teacher is cutting paper, she might say, "I cut the paper. Cut, cut the paper." This technique of self-talk also gives the child an opportunity to hear more mature phrases, sentences, and vocabulary. Some simple rules need to be followed when using this method: Teachers need to speak in simple, short phrases; describe their actions and thoughts; and not expect the children to directly imitate them. Self-talk and parallel talk allow children to hear models of more complex language and to realize that language is fun and useful (Lowenthal, 1995).

Classroom Interventions for Improvement of Pragmatics

The pragmatics of language or its use in social situations may be especially difficult for children who are maltreated to learn because of their lack of experience and/or their negative social interactions with their caregivers who are abusive or neglectful. Some teaching techniques to improve pragmatics involve motivating the children to appropriately use language in their interactions with others in the classroom. These strategies include the following (Cook, Tessier, & Klein, 1996; Rice, 1995):

- *The use of language for peer interactions:* This strategy focuses on the child's desire to play with other children, to tell his or her peers what to do, and to verbally express his or her intentions. The teacher encourages the child to communicate with others during play and models nonverbal aspects of pragmatics, such as turn taking, eye contact, and appropriate body language.
- *The use of language to get assistance:* This strategy capitalizes on the child's need for help in obtaining a desired toy, game, or other classroom material. The teacher reinforces the child's attempts to communicate by providing the material after a verbal request by the child.
- *The use of language to tell about activities:* This strategy requires that the teacher be an active listener. For example, when a child relates what is interesting to him or her, the teacher can listen attentively to encourage the child to talk more about the activities.
- *The use of language as a defense against peer aggression:* This strategy requires that the teachers model with words how to prevent a peer's aggression. The child is told to say "stop" rather than physically hitting or shoving the peer.

All of these strategies can be ways for teachers to improve the area of pragmatics in the language development of children who are abused and neglected.

Activity-Based Intervention

Activity-based intervention is an approach developed by Bricker (1998) that utilizes natural language instruction by the teacher. Bricker defined activity-based intervention as "a child-directed, transactional approach that embeds children's individual goals and objectives in routine, planned, or child-initiated activities and uses logically occurring antecedents and consequences to develop functional and generative skills" (p. 11). This approach can be especially beneficial for the language development of children who are abused and neglected because it encourages their participation in conversations as they are engaged in everyday activities. Caregivers who are abusive may discourage these conversations at home and prefer their children to be quiet and not bother them. Child-directed transactions require the teacher to attend to the child's interest or activity. The teacher joins the child and converses about the activity. Language stimulation is embedded or carried out during the typical routines of the day. Specific language goals are addressed, such as learning how to request something. For example, during snack time, the children are encouraged to ask for more juice or crackers if they want them. The antecedents for this request would be the juice and crackers on the table. The consequence would be that after making the requests, the children would get the juice or crackers. The goal of learning how to request something could then easily generalize to other daily activities (Bricker, 1993).

Peer-Mediated Intervention

Peer-mediated intervention involves the training of peers who do not have language delays to help the children who are maltreated with language difficulties to communicate more during the school day. The peer trainers are taught communicative strategies, such as establishing eye contact, initiating play and conversation, prompting the child with language delays to request turns, repeating and expanding the target child's language, describing the child's activity, and requesting clarification of unclear statements (Goldstein & Kaczmarek, 1992). The peer trainers may need to be periodically reminded to continue using prompts when they interact with the children who are maltreated. The teachers monitor the children's interactions and suggest strategies for the peer trainers to try. The teachers can give verbal prompts when necessary. Peer intervention can provide models for children who are maltreated to facilitate their learning of new social and communicative skills. It also can easily generalize from one environment to another (e.g., from the classroom to the playground) (Goldstein & Strain, 1994).

Teaching Techniques to Improve Listening Skills

Children who have been psychologically abused may have difficulties with their listening skills at school. Because of the harsh criticisms of them by their caregivers who are abusive, they may "tune out" or not listen as a defense mechanism. Teaching techniques to facilitate their listening skills and especially their abilities to follow directions follow (Orlich et al., 1998; Yehle & Rambold, 1998):

1. Give directions one at a time, and ask the students to repeat them. If needed, the teacher also should repeat them in a calm tone of voice.
2. Make the directions short and simple.
3. Provide both oral and written directions.
4. Use visual aides and pictures to reinforce listening skills.
5. Alert the students to pay attention to important information through cues (e.g., "Listen, you will need to know this").
6. Praise the students for listening carefully and following directions.

STRATEGIES FOR WRITTEN LANGUAGE DEVELOPMENT

Because of their difficulties with oral language, children who are maltreated also may have problems with their written language, which includes learning how to read and written expression. Word decoding skills may be an area in which they need assistance as it requires the association of the sounds of language with the letters of the alphabet. A structured, multisensory approach (e.g., the Orton-Gillingham method) could improve their decoding skills (Lerner, 2000). A description of this method follows.

The Orton-Gillingham Method

The Orton-Gillingham method (Gillingham & Stillman, 1997) focuses on teaching both reading decoding and spelling. At first, the children learn individual sounds and then blend them. They trace over the letters as they say the associated sounds and blends. In this way, their learning is reinforced through visual, auditory, and tactile channels. The sounds are then combined into syllables and later into words. Spelling is practical; the children write the letters of the words and say the sounds in the correct sequence for accurate spelling. This method can be adapted to meet the needs of younger and older students who are abused and neglected who have severe difficulties in learning to read and spell (Vaughn et al., 2000).

Bibliotherapy and Journal Writing

Two other selected therapeutic methods for improving written language skills and enhancing socioemotional development are bibliotherapy and journal writing. Bibliotherapy is a technique that encourages the reading of books that describe how children and adults overcame adversities and achieved success and happiness in their lives. Not only does bibliotherapy encourage reading skills, but it also gives hope to students who are at risk that they can solve their problems and that their futures will be brighter than the present (Lerner, 2000).

The second technique makes use of journal writing for the purposes of helping children who are maltreated with their skills in written expression and also in the socioemotional area of development. By keeping personal journals, the students practice their skills and also have the opportunity to express repressed feelings in appropriate ways by writing about them. The journals are confidential, and the students can choose to share or not to share their contents. Thus, they can feel safe from possible retaliation by caregivers who are abusive when negative comments are written about them.

INSTRUCTION IN MATHEMATICS

Some children who are maltreated have difficulty with mathematics. The reasons for this lack of achievement are thought to be due to these children's underlying socioemotional difficulties, which adversely affect their problem-solving and reasoning abilities required for success in this subject (Barnett, Vondra, & Shank, 1996; Beeghy & Cicchetti, 1994; Kurtz et al., 1993). In addition, their motivation to engage in and solve challenging tasks in this subject could be decreased (Barnett, 1997; Eckenrode et al., 1993; Vondra et al., 1990).

Some recommended principles of instruction that can assist these students are for the teachers to keep in mind that the understanding of mathematics progresses from the concrete to abstract levels, knowledge of this subject builds from incomplete comprehension to more complete understanding, and the thought process moves from unsystematic to systematic thinking. Therefore, mathematics should be taught in a predictable, structured sequence to facilitate its comprehension in students who are maltreated who have learning difficulties in this subject (Miller, Butler, & Lee, 1998).

The first step in the sequence is to teach at the concrete level in which manipulatives are used, such as toothpicks, poker chips, blocks, or other available objects in the classroom. The students work out solutions to problems by manipulating these materials, seeing the results, and talking about their answers. Thus, a multi-sensory approach facilitates their understanding of the process involved. After mastery at this level, the instruction moves to the semiconcrete stage at which the students represent the problems by pictures or marks on the paper. Following this, mathematics is taught at the abstract level in which numbers and other symbols are used. This stage can be the most difficult one for children who are maltreated to master because of the systematic reasoning and logic required. Caregivers who are neglectful or abusive in chaotic, disorganized home environments may not model this type of thought for them.

To assist these students with their abstract thinking and improve their motivation to achieve in mathematics, the National Council of Teachers of Mathematics (1991) and Vaughn et al. (2000) have made the following recommendations for teachers:

1. Provide many experiences for the students to apply mathematics to solving problems in everyday life. These activities improve their motivation to learn this subject.
2. Instruct the students when exact answers are necessary and when just estimation will suffice.
3. Teach the value and applications of calculators and computers in solving problems in mathematics.
4. Model systematic thinking and reasoning aloud so that the students better understand the process.
5. Adapt and/or modify the curriculum to meet their individual needs.

Other teaching tips are that teachers should place an emphasis on problem solving rather than on too much rote practice and drill and that they should provide immediate feedback on errors as well as positive reinforcement for efforts and success (Bos & Vaughn, 1998). Success in mathematics for students who are maltreated can be fostered when they are systematically taught at their developmental levels and when they are motivated to achieve by realizing that mathematics is a functional life skill.

CONCLUSION

This final chapter has described methods of teaching and instructional strategies that can assist children who are maltreated to learn and succeed at school. With fervent hope and intervention, teachers can work to make a positive difference in these children's lives. The teachers' visions are that their students realize their potentials in life-long learning; have nurturing, loving families; fulfill their childhood dreams; and become productive caring adults.

REFERENCES

Abrahams, N., Casey, K., & Daro, D. (1992). Teacher knowledge, attitudes, and beliefs about child abuse and its prevention. *Child Abuse and Neglect, 16,* 229–238.

Abruscato, J. (1994). Boost your students' social skills with this 9 step plan. *Learning, 22*(5), 60–66.

Adler, A. (1964). *Social interest.* New York: Capricorn Books.

Allan, J. (1994). Parenting education in Australia. *Children and Society, 8*(4), 344–359.

Allen, L., & Majidi-Ahi, S. (1989). Black American children. In J. Taylor Gibbs & L. Huang-Naheme (Eds.), *Children of color: Psychological interventions with minority youth* (pp. 148–178). San Francisco: Jossey-Bass.

Altepeter, T.S., & Walker, C.E. (1992). Prevention of physical abuse of children through parent training. In D.J. Willis, E.W. Holden, & M. Rosenberg (Eds.), *Prevention of child maltreatment: Developmental and ecological perspectives* (pp. 226–248). New York: John Wiley & Sons.

American Humane Association. (1998). *Children's division.* Englewood, CO: Author.

American Psychiatric Association. (1994). *Diagnostic and statistical manual of mental disorders* (4th ed.). Washington, DC: Author.

Ammerman, R.T., & Baladerian, N.J. (1993). *Maltreatment of children with disabilities.* Paper #860 presented at the National Committee for Prevention of Child Abuse, Chicago.

Ammerman, R.T., Lubetsky, M.J., & Drudy, K.F. (1991). Maltreatment of handicapped children. In R.T. Ammerman & M. Hersen (Eds.), *Case studies in family violence* (pp. 209–230). New York: Plenum Publishing.

Amster, B.J. (1999). Speech and language development of young children in the child welfare system. In J.A. Silver, B.J. Amster, & T. Haecker (Eds.), *Young children and foster care: A guide for professionals* (pp. 117–138). Baltimore: Paul H. Brookes Publishing Co.

Anastasiow, N., & Nucci, C. (1994). Social, historical, and theoretical special education and early intervention. In P.L. Safford (Ed.), *Early childhood special education* (pp. 7–25). New York: Teachers College Press.

Anderson, E.A., & Koblinsky, S.A. (1995). Homeless policy: The need to speak to families. *Family Relations, 44,* 13–18.

Au, K.H., & Kawakami, A.J. (1991). Culture and ownership. *Childhood Education, 67,* 280–284.

Bailey, D.B., Jr. (1996). An overview of interdisciplinary training. In D. Bricker & A. Widerstrom (Eds.), *Preparing personnel to work with infants and young children and their families: A team approach* (pp. 3–21). Baltimore: Paul H. Brookes Publishing Co.

Barnett, D. (1997). The effects of early intervention on maltreating parents and their children. In M.J. Guralnick (Ed.), *The effectiveness of early intervention* (pp. 147–170). Baltimore: Paul H. Brookes Publishing Co.

Barnett, D., Vondra, J.I., & Shonk, S. (1996). Relations among self-perceptions, motivation, and school functioning of low-income maltreated and non-maltreated children. *Child Abuse and Neglect, 20,* 397–410.

Barry, R.C., & Weber, T.R. (1994). Thoracoabdominal injuries associated with child abuse. In J.A. Monteleone & A.E. Brodeur (Eds.), *Child maltreatment: A clinical guide and reference* (pp. 57–66). St. Louis: G.W. Medical Publishing.

Bearcrane, J., Dodd, J.M., Nelson, J.R., & Ostwald, S.W. (1990). Educational characteristics of Native Americans. *Rural Educator, 11,* 1–5.

Beaty, J.J. (1999). *Prosocial guidance for the preschool child.* Upper Saddle River, NJ: Prentice Hall.

Becker, J.V. (1994). Offenders: Characteristics and treatment. *The Future of Children, 4*(2), 176–197.

Beckman, P.J. (1996). Theoretical, philosophical, and empirical bases of effective work with families. In P.J. Beckman (Ed.), *Strategies for working with families of young children with disabilities* (pp. 1–16). Baltimore: Paul H. Brookes Publishing Co.

Beeghly, M., & Cicchetti, D. (1994). Child maltreatment, attachment, and the self system: Emergence of an internal state lexicon in toddlers at high social risk. *Development and Psychopathology, 6,* 5–30.

Bender, W.N., Rosenkrans, C.B., & Crane, M.K. (1999). Stress, depression, and suicide among students with learning disabilities: Assessing the risk. *Learning Disability Quarterly, 22,* 143–156.

Bennett, T., Lingerfelt, B.V., & Nelson, D.E. (1990). *Developing individualized family support plans.* Cambridge, MA: Brookline Books.

Berger, E.H. (1991). *Parents as partners in education: The school and home working together.* Upper Saddle River, NJ: Prentice Hall.

Berger, E.H. (2000). *Parents as partners in education: Families and schools working together.* Upper Saddle River, NJ: Prentice Hall.

Besharov, D.J. (1990). *Recognizing child abuse: A guide for the concerned.* New York: The Free Press.

Besharov, D.J. (1994). Responding to sexual abuse: The need for a balanced approach. *The Future of Children, 4*(2), 135–155.

Bos, C.S., & Vaughn, S. (1998). *Teaching students with learning and behavior problems.* Needham Heights, MA: Allyn & Bacon.

Boxer, A.M. (1992). Adolescent pregnancy and parenthood in the transition to adulthood. In M. Rosenheim & M.F. Testa (Eds.), *Early parenthood and coming of age in the 1990s* (pp. 46–54). New Brunswick, NJ: Rutgers University Press.

Bricker, D. (1993). Then, now, and the path between: A brief history of language intervention. In S.F. Warren & J. Reichle (Series Eds.) & A.P. Kaiser & D.B. Gray (Vol. Eds.), *Communication and language intervention series: Vol. 2. Enhancing children's communication: Research foundations for intervention* (pp. 11–31). Baltimore: Paul H. Brookes Publishing Co.

Bricker, D.D. (1998). *An activity-based approach to early intervention* (2nd ed.). Baltimore: Paul H. Brookes Publishing Co.

Briere, J., & Runtz, M. (1993). Childhood sexual abuse: Long-term sequelae and implication for psychological assessment. *Journal of Interpersonal Violence, 8*(3), 312–330.

Briere, J.N., & Elliot, D.M. (1994). Immediate and long-term impacts of child sexual abuse. *The Future of Children, 4*(2), 54–69.

Bronfenbrenner, Y. (1979). *The ecology of family development.* Cambridge, MA: Harvard University Press.

Brooks, C.S., & Rice, K.F. (1997). *Families in recovery: Coming full circle.* Baltimore: Paul H. Brookes Publishing Co.

Brooks, R. (1994). Children at-risk: Fostering resilience and hope. *American Journal of Orthopsychiatry, 64*(4), 545–553.

Bucci, J.A., & Reitzhammer, A.F. (1992). Collaboration with health and social service professionals: Preparing teachers for new roles. *Journal of Teacher Education, 43,* 290–295.

Bugental, D.B. (1992). Affective and cognitive processes within threat-oriented family systems. In I.E. Siegel, A.V. McGillicuddy-DeLisi, & J.J. Goodnow (Eds.), *Parental belief systems: The psychological consequences for children* (pp. 219–248). Mahwah, NJ: Lawrence Erlbaum Associates.

Burl, N.T. (1992). *Conversational abilities of maltreated children.* Unpublished doctoral dissertation. University of Memphis, Tennessee.

Buscemi, L., Bennett, T., Thomas, D., & Deluca, D. (1995). Head start: Challenges and training needs. *Journal of Early Intervention, 20*(1), 1–13.

Carmody, M. (1991). Invisible victims: Sexual assault of people with an intellectual disability. *Australia and New Zealand Journal of Developmental Disabilities, 17,* 229–236.

Case, M.E.S. (1994). Head injury in child abuse. In J.A. Monteleone and A.E. Brodeur (Eds.), *Child maltreatment: A clinical guide and reference* (pp. 75–87). St. Louis: G.W. Medical Publishing.

Chan, S. (1998). Families with Asian roots. In E.W. Lynch & M.J. Hanson (Eds.), *Developing cross-cultural competence: A guide for working with children and their families* (2nd ed., pp. 251–354). Baltimore: Paul H. Brookes Publishing Co.

Chao, C.M. (1992). The inner heart: Therapy with Southeast Asian families. In L.A. Vargas & J.D. Koss-Chioino (Eds.), *Working with culture: Psychotherapeutic interventions with ethnic minority children and adolescents* (pp. 157–181). San Francisco: Jossey-Bass.

Child Abuse Prevention and Treatment Act (CAPTA) of 1974, PL 93-247, 42 U.S.C. §§ 5101 *et seq.*

Christian, C.W. (1999). Child abuse and neglect. In J.A. Silver, B.J. Amster, & T. Haecker (Eds.), *Young children and foster care: A guide for professionals* (pp. 195–212). Baltimore: Paul H. Brookes Publishing Co.

Cicchetti, D., Toth, S.L., & Hennessy, A. (1989). Research on the consequences of child maltreatment and its application to educational settings. *Topics in Early Childhood Special Education, 9*(2), 33–55.

Cole, C.K. (1995). Classroom interventions for young children at risk. In G. Harold Smith, E.C. Coles, M.K. Poulsen, & C.K. Cole (Eds.), *Children, families, and substance abuse: Challenges for changing educational and social outcomes* (pp. 121–153). Baltimore: Paul H. Brookes Publishing Co.

Cook, R.E., Tessier, A., & Klein, M.D. (1996). *Adapting early childhood curricula for children in inclusive settings* (4th ed.). Upper Saddle River, NJ: Prentice Hall.

Cook, R.E., Tessier, A., & Klein, M.D. (2000). *Adapting early childhood curricula for children in inclusive settings* (5th ed.). Upper Saddle River, NJ: Prentice Hall.

Cooney, J. (1991). Counseling and child abuse: A developmental perspective. In J. Carlson & J. Lewis (Eds.), *Family counseling strategies and issues* (pp. 225–242). Denver, CO: Love Publishing.

Cooper, C.S., Dunst, C.J., & Vance, S.D. (1990). The effect of social support on adolescent mothers' styles of parent-child interaction as measured in three separate occasions. *Adolescence, 25*, 49–57.

Copeland, A., & White, K.M. (1991). *Studying families.* Beverly Hills: Sage Publications.

Coster, W., & Cicchetti, D.J. (1993). Research on the communicative development of maltreated children: Clinical implications. *Topics in Language Disorders, 13*, 25–38.

Crais, E.R. (1996). Applying family-centered principles to child assessment. In P.J. McWilliam, P.J. Winton, & E.R. Crais (Eds.), *Practice strategies for family-centered intervention* (pp. 69–96). San Diego: Singular Publishing Group.

Crittenden, P.M. (1996). Research on maltreating families: Implications for intervention. In J. Briere, L. Berliner, J.A. Bulkley, C. Jenny, & T. Reid (Eds.), *The APSAC handbook on child maltreatment* (pp. 158–174). Beverly Hills: Sage Publications.

Culp, R.E., Little, V., Letts, D., & Lawrence, H. (1991). Maltreated children's self-concept. Effect of a comprehensive treatment program. *American Journal of Orthopsychiatry, 61*, 114–121.

Daro, D. (1993). Child maltreatment research: Implications for program design. In D. Cicchetti & S. Toth (Eds.), *Child abuse, child development, and social policy* (pp. 331–367). Norwood, NJ: Ablex.

DePanfilis, D. (1996). Social isolation of neglectful families: A review of social support assessment and intervention models. *Child Maltreatment, 1*(1), 38–52.

Department of Health and Human Services, Administration for Children and Families, U.S. Advisory Board on Abuse and Neglect. (1993, April). *The continuing child protection emergency: A challenge to the nation.* Washington, DC: U.S. Government Printing Office.

DeSantis, L.D., & Thomas, J.T. (1994). Childhood independence: Views of Cuban and Haitian immigrant mothers. *Journal of Pediatric Nursing, 9*, 258–267.

Dinkmeyer, D., & McKay, G.D. (1989). *STEP: Systematic training for effective parenting.* Circle Pines, MN: American Guidance Service.

Dinkmeyer, D., Sr., McKay, G.D., & Dinkmeyer, D., Jr. (1990). Inaccuracy in STEP research reporting. *Canadian Journal of Counseling, 24*, 103–105.

Dodge, K., Pettit, G., & Bates, J. (1994). Effects of physical maltreatment on the development of peer relations. *Development and Psychopathology, 6*, 43–55.

Donahue-Kilburg, G. (1992). *Family-centered intervention for communication disorders.* Rockville, MD: Aspen Publishers.

Dryfoos, J.G. (1994). *Full service schools.* San Francisco: Jossey-Bass.

Dunst, C.J., Trivette, C.M., & Deal, A.G. (1994). Enabling and empowering families. In C.J. Dunst, C.M. Trivette, & A.G. Deal (Eds.), *Supporting and strengthening families* (pp. 2–11). Cambridge, MA: Brookline Books.

Dunst, C.J., Trivette, C.M., & Jodry, W. (1997). Influences of social support on children with disabilities and their families. In M.J. Guralnick (Ed.), *The effectiveness of early intervention* (pp. 499–522). Baltimore: Paul H. Brookes Publishing Co.

Eckenrode, J., Laird, M., & Doris, J. (1993). School performance and disciplinary problems among abused and neglected children. *Developmental Psychology, 29*, 53–62.

Egeland, B. (1998, February 23–25). The consequences of physical and emotional neglect on the development of young children. In U.S. Department of Health and Human Services, Office of Human Development Services, Administration on Children, Youth and Families, Children's Bureau, *National Center on Child Abuse and Neglect: Research symposium on child neglect.* D-10–D-21.

Elksnin, L.K., & Elksnin, N. (1998). Teaching social skills to students with learning and behavior problems. *Intervention in School and Clinic, 33*(3), 131–140.

England, S.P., & Sundberg, S. (1996). Management of common pediatric fractures. *Pediatric Clinics of North America, 43*(5), 991–1012.

Erickson, M.F., Stroufe, L.A., & Pianta, R. (1989). The effects of maltreatment on the development of young children. In D. Cicchetti & V. Carson (Eds.), *Child maltreatment: Theory and research on the consequences of abuse and neglect* (pp. 647–684). New York: Cambridge University Press.

Erikson, E. (1968). *Identity, youth, and crisis.* New York: W.W. Norton and Company.

Family Support Act (FSA) of 1988, PL 100-48, 42 U.S.C. §§ 1305 *et seq.*

Farmer, T.W., Farmer, M.Z., & Gut, D.M. (1999). Implications for social development research for school-based interventions for aggressive youth with EBD. *Journal of Emotional and Behavioral Disorders, 7*(3), 130–136.

Fennimore, B.S. (1989). *Child advocacy for early childhood educators.* New York: Teachers College Press.

Ferber, J. (1996). A look in the mirror: Self-concept in preschool children. In L. Koplow (Ed.), *Unsmiling faces: How preschools can heal* (pp. 27–42) New York: Teachers College Press.

Fiedler, C.R. (2000). *Making a difference: Advocacy competencies for special education professionals.* Needham Heights, MA: Allyn & Bacon.

Finkelhor, D., & Dzuiba-Leatherman, J. (1994). Children as victims of violence: A national survey. *Pediatrics, 94*(4), 413–420.

Fisher, J., Schumaker, J., & Deshler, D. (1995). Searching for validated inclusion practice: A review of the literature. *Focus on Exceptional Children, 28*(4), 1–20.

Franca, V.M., Kerr, M.M., Reitz, A.L., & Lambert, D. (1990). Peer tutoring among behaviorally disordered students: Academic and social benefits to tutor and tutee. *Education and Treatment of Children, 13*, 109–128.

Friend, M., & Cook, L. (1992). *Interactions: Collaboration skills for school professionals.* White Plains, NY: Longman.

Fuchs, D., & Fuchs, L. (1998). Researchers and teachers working together to adapt instruction for diverse learners. *Learning Disabilities: Research and Practice, 13*(3), 126–137.

Fuchs, D., Fuchs, L.S., & Burish, A. (2000). Peer-assisted learning strategies: An evidence-based practice to promote reading achievement. *Learning Disabilities Research and Practice, 15*(2), 85–91.

Furniss, T. (1991). *The multi-professional handbook of child sexual abuse: Integrated management, therapy, and legal intervention.* London: Routledge.

Gallagher, T.M. (1991). Language and social skills: Implications for clinical assessment and intervention with school-age children. In T.M. Gallagher (Ed.), *Pragmatics of language: Clinical practice issues* (pp. 11–41). San Diego: Singular Publishing Group.

Garcia, E.E. (1992). Linguistically and culturally diverse children: Effective instructional practices and related policy issues. In H.C. Waxman, J.W. deFelix, J.E. Anderson, & H.P. Batiste, Jr. (Eds.), *Students at-risk in at-risk schools: Improving environments for learning* (pp. 65–86). Beverly Hills: Sage Publications.

Gardner, H. (1993). *Multiple intelligences: The theory in practice.* New York: John Wiley & Sons.

Gaudin, J.M. (1993). Effective intervention with neglectful families. *Criminal Justice and Behavior, 20,* 66–89.

Gelles, R. (1993). Family reunification/family preservation: Are children really being protected? *Journal of Interpersonal Violence, 8*(4), 557–562.

Gelles, R.J., & Lancaster, J.B. (1987). *Child abuse and neglect: Biosocial dimension.* New York: Aldine de Gruyter.

Gillingham, A., & Stillman, B.W. (1997). *The Gillingham manual: Remedial training for children with specific disability in reading, writing, and penmanship* (8th ed.). Cambridge, MA: Educators Publishing Service.

Glasgow, J.H., & Adaskin, E.J. (1990). The West Indians. In N. Waxler-Morrison, J. Anderson, & E. Richardson (Eds.), *Cross-cultural caring: A handbook for health professionals in Western Canada* (pp. 214–244). Vancouver: University of British Columbia Press

Goens, G.A. (1996, October). Shared decisions, empowerment, and ethics: Admission impossible for district leaders? *The School Administrator,* 12–14.

Goldstein, H., & Kaczmarek, L. (1992). Promoting communicative interaction among children in integrated intervention settings. In S.F. Warren & J. Reichle (Series & Vol. Eds.), *Communication and language intervention series: Vol 1. Causes and effects in communication and language intervention* (pp. 81–111). Baltimore: Paul H. Brookes Publishing Co.

Goldstein, H., & Strain, P.S. (1994). Peers as communication agents: Some new strategies and research findings. In K.G. Butler (Ed.), *Early intervention: Working with parents and families* (pp. 110–112). Rockville, MD: Aspen Publishers.

Gondolf, E.W. (1995). *Men who batter.* Homes Beach, FL: Learning Publications.

Gootman, M. (1993). Reaching and teaching abused children. *Childhood Education, 70,* 15–19.

Gordon, T. (1975). *P.E.T.: Parent effectiveness training.* New York: Wyden.

Graden, J.L., & Bauer, A.M. (1992). Using a collaborative approach to support students and teachers in inclusive classrooms. In S. Stainback & W. Stainback (Eds.), *Curriculum considerations in inclusive classrooms: Facilitating learning for all students* (pp. 85–100). Baltimore: Paul H. Brookes Publishing Co.

Greenspan, S., & Negron, E. (1994). Ethical obligations of special services personnel. *Special Services in the Schools, 8*(2), 185–209.

Greenwood, C.R. (1996). Research on the practices and behavior of effective teachers at the Juniper Gardens Child's Project: Implication for the education of diverse learners. In D.L. Speece & B. Keogh (Eds.), *Research on classroom ecologies: Implications for inclusion of children with learning disabilities* (pp. 39–67). Mahwah, NJ: Lawrence Erlbaum Associates.

Greenwood, C.R., & Terry, B. (1997, June). *Classwide peer tutoring.* Paper presented at the 20th annual Intervention Procedures Conference for At-Risk Children and Youth, Utah State University, Logan.

Greis, S.M. (1999). Feeding disorders in young children. In J.A. Silver, B.J. Amster, &T. Haecker (Eds.), *Young children and foster care: A guide for professionals* (pp. 65–91). Baltimore: Paul H. Brookes Publishing Co.

Groce, N. (1990). Comparative and cross-cultural issues. *Disability Studies Quarterly, 10,* 1–39.

Groce, N.E., & Zola, I.K. (1993). Multiculturalism, chronic illness, and disability. *Pediatrics, 91,* 1048–1055.

Gunnar, M., Broderson, R.L., Krueger, K., & Rigatuso, R. (1996). Dampening of behavioral and adrenocortical reactivity during early infancy: Normative changes and individual differences. *Child Development, 67*(3), 877–889.

Guralnick, M.J. (1992). A hierarchial model for understanding children's peer-related social competence. In S.L. Odom, S.R. McConnell, & M.A. McEvoy (Eds.), *Social competence of young children with disabilities: Issues and strategies for intervention* (pp. 37–64). Baltimore: Paul. H. Brookes Publishing Co.

Haager, D., & Vaughn S. (1995). Parent, teacher, peer, and self-reports of the social competence of students with learning disabilities. *Journal of Learning Disabilities, 28*(4), 205–215.

Halfon, N., Mendonca, A., & Berkowitz, G. (1995). Health status of children in foster care: The experience of the Center for Vulnerable Children. *Archives of Pediatric and Adolescent Medicine, 194,* 386–392.

Hamburg, B.A., & Dixon, S.L. (1992). Adolescent pregnancy and parenthood. In M. Rosenheim & M.F. Testa (Eds.), *Early parenthood and coming of age in the 1990's* (pp. 17–33). New Brunswick, NJ: Rutgers University Press.

Hanson, M.J., & Lynch, E.W. (1992). Family diversity: Implications for policy and practice. *Topics in Early Childhood Special Education, 12*(3), 283–306.

Hanson, M.J., & Lynch, E.W. (1995). *Early intervention: Implementing child and family services for infants and toddlers who are at-risk or disabled.* Austin, TX: PRO-ED.

Harper, G.F., Mallette, B., & Moore, J. (1991). Peer-mediated instruction: Teaching spelling to primary school children with mild disabilities. *Journal of Reading, Writing, and Learning Disabilities International, 7*(3), 137–151.

Harry, B. (1992). Developing cultural self-awareness: The first step in values clarification for early interventionists. *Topics in Early Childhood Special Education, 12*(3), 333–350.

Hegar, R., & Scannapieco, M. (1995). From family duty to family policy: The evaluation of kinship care. *Child Welfare, 75,* 200–217.

Herman, J. (1992). *Trauma and recovery.* New York: Basic Books.

Heron, T.E., Martz, S.A., & Margolis, H. (1996). Ethical and legal issues in consultation. *Remedial and Special Education, 17*(6), 377–385.

Hildebrand, V., Phenice, L.A., Gray, M.M., & Hines, R.P. (2000). *Knowing and serving diverse families.* Upper Saddle River, NJ: Prentice Hall.

Hodgkinson, H.L. (1989). *The same client: The demographics of education and service delivery systems.* Washington, DC: Institute for Educational Leadership. (ERIC Document Reproduction Service No. ED312757.)

Horner, R.H., & Carr, E.G. (1997). Behavioral support for students with severe disabilities: Functional assessment and comprehensive intervention. *Journal of Special Education, 31,* 81–104.

Howard, V.F., Williams, B.F., Port, P.D., & Lepper, C. (1997). *Very young children with special needs.* Upper Saddle River, NJ: Prentice Hall.

Hughes, C.A. (1996). Memory and test-taking strategies. In D.D. Deshler, E.S. Ellis, & B.K. Lenz (Eds.), *Teaching adolescents with learning disabilities: Strategies and methods* (2nd ed., pp. 209–266). Denver, CO: Love Publishing.

Hunt, N., & Marshall, K. (1999). *Exceptional children and youth.* Boston: Houghton Mifflin Co.

Hurd, T.L., Lerner, R.M., & Alten, C.E. (1999). Integrated services: Expanding partnerships to meet the needs of today's children and families. *Young Children, 54*(2), 74–80.

Individuals with Disabilities Education Act (IDEA) Amendments of 1997, PL 105-17, 20 U.S.C. §§ 1400 *et seq.*

James, B. (1994). *Handbook for treatment of attachment: Trauma problems in children.* New York: Lexington Books.

Janney, R., & Snell, M.E. (2000). *Behavioral support.* Baltimore: Paul H. Brookes Publishing Co.

Jaudes, P.K., & Shapiro, L.D. (1999). Child abuse and developmental disabilities. In J.A. Silver, B.J. Amster, & T. Haecker (Eds.), *Young children and foster care: A guide for professionals* (pp. 213–234). Baltimore: Paul H. Brookes Publishing Co.

Joe, J.R., & Malach, R.S. (1998). Families with Native American roots. In E.W. Lynch & M.J. Hanson (Eds.), *Developing cross-cultural competence: A guide for working with children and their families* (2nd ed., pp. 127–164). Baltimore: Paul H. Brookes Publishing Co.

Johnson, D.W., & Johnson, R.T. (1995). *Teaching students to be peacemakers.* Edina, MN: Interaction Book Company.

Johnson, D.W., & Johnson, R.T. (1996). Conflict resolution and peer mediation programs in elementary and secondary schools: A review of the research. *Review of Educational Research, 66*(4), 459–506.

Johnson, D.W., & Johnson, R.T. (1996). Cooperative learning and traditional American values: An appreciation. *NASSP Bulletin, 80*(579), 63–65.

Johnson, D.W., & Johnson, R.T. (1998). Teaching students to manage conflicts in diverse classrooms. In J.W. Putnam (Ed.), *Cooperative learning and strategies for inclusion: Celebrating diversity in the classroom* (2nd ed., pp. 167–184). Baltimore: Paul H. Brookes Publishing Co.

Kagan, S. (1995). *Cooperative learning.* San Clemente, CA: Kagan Cooperative Learning.

Kagan, S. (1998). *Multiple intelligences.* San Clemente, CA: Kagan Cooperative Learning.

Kaiser, A.P., & Hester, P.P. (1994). Generalized effects of enhanced milieu teaching. *Journal of Speech and Hearing Research, 37,* 1320–1340.

Katz, M. (1997). Overcoming childhood adversities: Lessons learned from those who have "beat the odds." *Intervention in School and Clinic, 32*(4), 205–210.

Kemp, A. (1998). *Abuse in the family: An introduction.* Pacific Grove, CA: Brooks/Cole Publishing.

Kempe, C.H., Silverman, F.N., Steele, B.F., Droegmuller, W., & Silver, H.K. (1962). The battered child syndrome. *Journal of the American Medical Association, 181*(1), 17–24.

Koplow, L. (1996). Therapeutic technique: The tools of preschools that heal. In L. Koplow (Ed.), *Unsmiling faces: How preschools can heal* (pp. 89–105). New York: Teachers College Press.

Kurtz, P.D., Jaudin, J.M., Wodarski, J.S., & Howling, P.T. (1993). Maltreatment and the school-aged child: School performance consequences. *Child Abuse and Neglect, 17,* 581–589.

Lambie, R. (2000). *Family systems within educational contexts.* Denver, CO: Love Publishing.

Lambie, R. (2000). *Understanding at-risk and special-needs students.* Denver, CO: Love Publishing.

Landes, A., Siegel, M.A., & Foster, C.D. (1993). *Domestic violence: No longer behind the curtains.* Wylie, TX: Information Plus.

Larson, C.S., Gumby, D.S., Shiono, P.H., Lewit, E.M., & Behrman, R.E. (1992). Analysis. *The Future of Children, 2,* 6–18.

LeDoux, J.E. (1992). Brain mechanisms of emotion and emotional learning. *Current Opinion in Neurobiology, 2*(2), 1991–1997.

Lequerica, M. (1993). Stress in immigrant families with handicapped children: A child advocacy approach. *American Journal of Orthopsychiatry, 63,* 545–552.

Lerner, J.W. (2000). *Learning disabilities: Theories, diagnosis, and teaching strategies.* Boston: Houghton Mifflin Co.

Lerner, J.W., Lowenthal, B., & Egan, R. (1998). *Preschool children with special needs: Children at-risk, children with disabilities.* Needham Heights, MA: Allyn & Bacon.

Lerner, J.W., Lowenthal, B., & Lerner, S. (1995). *Attention deficit disorders: Assessment and teaching.* Pacific Grove, CA: Brooks/Cole Publishing.

Leung, B. (1996). Is the court-appointed special advocate program effective? A longitudinal analysis of time involvement and case outcomes. *Child Welfare, LXXV*(3), 269–282.

Lewitt, E.M. (1994). Reported child abuse and neglect. *The Future of Children, 4*(2), 233–242.

Lieberman, A.F., Weston, D.R., & Pawl, J.H. (1991). Preventive intervention and outcome with anxiously attached dyads. *Child Development, 62,* 199–209.

Lindsey, D. (1994). Family preservation and child protection: Striking a balance. *Children and Youth Review, 16*(5), 279–294.

Litow, M. (1996). *Fact sheet.* Oak Park, IL: Education Center.

Lopez, L. (1999, Fall). The seven A's of self-esteem. *Learning Disability Association-United Chapter Newsletter*, 3–4.

Lowenthal, B. (1995). Naturalistic language intervention in inclusive environments. *Intervention in School and Clinic, 31*, 114–118.

Lowenthal, B. (1996). Educational implications of child abuse. *Intervention in School and Clinic, 32*(1), 21–25.

Lowenthal, B. (1996). The effects of early childhood abuse and the development of resiliency. *Early Child Development and Care, 142*, 43–52.

Lowenthal, B. (1998). Educational implications of child abuse. *Intervention in School and Clinic, 32*(1), 21–25.

Lowenthal, B., & Lowenthal, R. (1997). Teenage parenting: Challenges, interventions, and programs. *Childhood Education, 74*(1), 29–32.

Lynch, E.W. (1998). Conceptual framework: From culture shock to cultural learning. In E.W. Lynch & M.J. Hanson (Eds.), *Developing cross-cultural competence: A guide for working with children and their families* (pp. 23–45). Baltimore: Paul H. Brookes Publishing Co.

MacIntyre, T. (1990). The teacher's role in cases of suspected child abuse. *Education and Urban Society, 22*(3), 300–306.

Mack, A.E., & Warr-Leeper, G.A. (1992). Language abilities in boys with chronic behavior disorders. *Language, Speech, and Hearing Services in Schools, 23*, 214–223.

Mahoney, G., & Neville-Smith, A. (1996). The effect of directive communications on children's interactive engagement: Implications for language development. Topics in *Early Childhood Special Education, 16*(2), 236–249.

Maldonado-Duran, M., & Saucida-Garcia, J.M. (1996). Excessive crying in infants with regulatory disorders. *Bulletin of the Menninger Clinic, 60*(1), 62–78.

Manly, J.T., Cicchetti, D., & Barnett, D. (1994). The impact of subtype, frequency, and chronicity, and severity of child maltreatment on social competence and behavior problems. *Developmental and Psychopathology, 6*, 121–143.

Marion, M. (1999). *Guidance of young children.* Upper Saddle River, NJ: Prentice Hall.

Mash, E.J., & Wolfe, D.A. (1991). Methodological issues in research in child abuse. *Criminal Justice and Behavior, 18*, 8–29.

Maslow, A. (1954). *Motivation and personality.* New York: Harper & Row.

Master, A.S., & Coatsworth, J.D. (1995). *Competence, resilience, and psychopathology: Risk, disorder, and adaptation* (Vol. 2, pp. 715–754). New York: John Wiley & Sons.

McCollum, J.A., & Yates, T.J. (1994). Dyad as focus, triad as means: A family-centered approach to supporting parent-child interactions. *Infants and Young Children, 6*(4), 54–63.

McCurdy, K., & Daro, D. (1994). *Current trends in child abuse reporting and fatalities: The results of the 1993 fifty-state survey.* Prepared by the National Center on Child Abuse Prevention Research. Chicago: National Committee for Prevention of Child Abuse.

McIntyre, T. (1990). The teacher's role in cases of suspected child abuse. *Education and Urban Society, 22*, 307–313.

McMillan, J., & Reed, D. (1993). At-risk students and resiliency: Factors contributing to academic success. *The Clearing House, 67*(3), 137–140.

Miller, S., Butler, F., & Lee, K. (1998). Validated practices for teaching mathematics to students with learning disabilities: A review of the literature. *Focus on Exceptional Children, 31*(1), 1–24.

Milner, J.S., & Chilamkurti, C. (1991). Physical child abuse perpetuator characteristics. *Journal of Interpersonal Violence, 6*(3), 345–366.

Monteleone, J.A., & Brodeur, A.E. (1994). Identifying, interpreting, and reporting injuries. In J.A. Monteleone & A.E. Brodeur (Eds.), *Child maltreatment: A clinical guide and reference* (pp. 1–26). St. Louis: G.W. Medical Publishing.

Moroz, K.J. (1993). *Supporting adoptive families with special needs children— A handbook for mental health professionals.* Waterbury: The Vermont Adoptions Project.

Moroz, K.J. (1996). *Mediating the effects of childhood trauma.* Oak Brook, IL: Sixth Annual Illinois Faculty Development Institute in Early Intervention (0–3).

Morrison, J.A., Frank, S.J., Holland, C.C., & Kates, W.R. (1999). Emotional development and disorders in young children in the child welfare system. In J.A. Silver, B.J. Amster, & T. Haecker (Eds.), *Young children and foster care: A guide for professionals* (pp. 33–64). Baltimore: Paul H. Brookes Publishing Co.

Munkel, W.I. (1994). Neglect and abandonment. In J.A. Monteleone & A.E. Brodeur (Eds.), *Child maltreatment: A clinical guide and reference* (pp. 241–257). St. Louis: G.W. Medical Publishing.

Musick, J.S. (1994). Grandmothers and grandmothers-to-be: Effects on adolescent mothers and adolescent mothering. *Infants and Young Children, 6*, 1–9.

Nash, J.M. (1997, February 3). Fertile minds. *Time, 3*, 48–56.

National Association for the Education of Young Children (NAEYC). (1998). What would you do? Real-life ethical problems early childhood professionals face. *Young Children, 53*, 53–54.

National Center on Child Abuse and Neglect (NCCAN). (1994). *Child maltreatment 1992: Reports from the states to the National Center on Child Abuse and Neglect.* Washington, DC: U.S. Government Printing Office.

National Center on Child Abuse and Neglect (NCCAN). (1995). *Child abuse and neglect fact sheet, 1993.* Washington, DC: U.S. Government Printing Office.

National Center on Child Abuse and Neglect (NCCAN). (1996). *Child abuse and neglect fact sheet, 1994.* Washington, DC: U.S. Government Printing Office.

National Center on Child Abuse and Neglect (NCCAN). (1996). *Child maltreatment 1994: Reports from the states to the National Center on Child Abuse and Neglect.* Washington, DC: U.S. Government Printing Office.

National Council of Teachers of Mathematics. (1991). *Professional standards for teaching mathematics.* Reston, VA: Author.

National Education Goals Panel. (1994). *The national education goals report: Building a nation of learners, executive summary.* Washington, DC: Author.

Nelson, R.A. (1994). Issues, communication, and advocacy: Contemporary ethical challenges. *Public Relations Review, 20*(3), 225–231.

Nevin, A. (1998). Curricular and instructional adaptations for including students with disabilities in cooperative groups. In J.W. Putnam (Ed.), *Co-*

operative learning and strategies for inclusion (2nd ed., pp. 49–66). Baltimore: Paul H. Brookes Publishing Co.

Newberger, J.J. (1997). Brain development research: A wonderful window of opportunity to build public support for early childhood education. *Young Children, 52*, 4–9.

Nunnelley, J.C., & Fields, T. (1999). Anger, dismay, guilt, anxiety: The realities and roles in reporting child abuse. *Young Children, 54*(5), 74–80.

O'Neill, R.E. (1997). Autism. In J.W. Wood & A.M. Lazzari (Eds.), *Exceeding the boundaries: Understanding exceptional lives* (pp. 424–461). San Diego: Harcourt Brace Jovanovich.

Olenick, M., & McCroskey, J. (1992). *Social and health services in Los Angeles County Schools: Countrywide data on available need and funding.* Los Angeles: Los Angeles Roundtable for Children and Los Angeles County Office of Education.

Orlich, D.C., Harder, R.J., Callahan, R.C., & Gibson, H.W. (1998). *Teaching strategies: A guide to better instruction.* Boston: Houghton Mifflin Co.

Osofsky, J.D., Hann, D.M., & Peebles, C. (1993). Adolescent parenthood: Risks and opportunities for mothers and infants. In C.H. Zeanah, Jr. (Ed.), *Handbook of infant mental health* (pp. 106–119). New York: The Guilford Press.

Ounce of Prevention Fund. (1996). *Starting smart: How early experiences affect brain development.* Chicago: Author.

Palincsar, H., & Klenk, L. (1992). Fostering literacy learning in supportive contexts. *Journal of Learning Disabilities, 25*, 211–225.

Pecora, P.J., Whittaker, J.K., & Maluccio, A.N. (1992). *The child welfare challenge.* New York: Aldine de Gruyter.

Perry, B.D. (1993). Medicine and psychotherapy: Neurodevelopment and neurophysiology of trauma. *The Advisor, 6*, 13–20.

Perry, B.D. (1996). *Maltreated children: Experience, brain development and the next generation.* New York: W.W. Norton and Company.

Perry, B.D., Pollard, R.A., Blakely, T.L., Baker, W.L., & Vigilante, D. (1995). Childhood trauma, the neurobiology of adaption, and "use-dependent" development of the brain: How "states" became traits. *Infant Mental Health Journal, 16*(4), 271–288.

Phillips, C.B. (1994). The movement of African-American children through sociocultural contexts: A case of conflict resolution. In B.L. Mallory & R.S. New (Eds.), *Diversity and developmentally appropriate practices* (pp. 137–154). New York: Teachers College Press.

Polansky, N.A., Chalmers, M.A., Buttenwieser, E., & Williams, D.P. (1987). *Damaged parents: An anatomy of child neglect.* Chicago: University of Chicago Press.

Popkin, M.H. (1989). Active Parenting: A video-based program. In M.J. Fine (Ed.), *The second handbook on parent education: Contemporary perspectives* (pp. 77–98). San Diego: Academic Press.

Premack, D. (1959). Toward empirical behavior law, 1: Positive reinforcement. *Pychological Review, 66*, 219–223.

Putnam, J.W. (1998). The process of cooperative learning. In J.W. Putnam (Ed.), *Cooperative learning and strategies for inclusion* (2nd ed., pp. 17–48). Baltimore: Paul H. Brookes Publishing Co.

Radford, N.T. (1998). Practical approaches for identifying and managing abused and neglected children. *Infant-Toddler Intervention, 8*(3), 287–304.

Reppucci, N.D., Britner, P.A., & Woolard, J.L. (1997). *Preventing child abuse and neglect through parent education.* Baltimore: Paul H. Brookes Publishing Co.

Reyome, N.D. (1993). A comparison of the school performance of sexually abused, neglected, and non-maltreated children. *Child Study Journal, 23,* 17–38.

Rice, M.L. (1995). The rationale and operating principles for a language-focused curriculum for preschool children. In M.L. Rice & K.A. Wilcox (Eds.), *Building a language-focused curriculum for the preschool classroom: A foundation for lifelong communication* (Vol. 1, pp. 27–38). Baltimore: Paul H. Brookes Publishing Co.

Rivers, K.O., & Hedrick, D.L. (1998). A follow-up study of language and behavioral concerns of children prenatally exposed to drugs. *Infant-Toddler Intervention, 8*(1), 29–51.

Robinson, S. (1990). *Putting the pieces together: Survey of state systems for children in crisis.* Denver, CO: National Conference of State Legislators.

Roundy, L.M., & Horton, A.L. (1991). Professional and treatment issues for clinicians who intervene with incest perpetrators. In A.L. Horton, B.L. Johnson, L.M. Roundy, & D. Williams (Eds.), *The incest perpetrator: A family member no one wants to treat* (pp. 164–189). Beverly Hills: Sage Publications.

Sabota, E.E., & Davis, R.L. (1992). Fatality after report to a child abuse registry in Washington state: 1973–1986. *Child Abuse and Neglect, 16,* 627–635.

Sagor, R. (1996). Building resiliency in students. *Educational Leadership, 54*(1), 38–43.

Salend, S.J. (1999). Facilitating friendships among diverse students. *Intervention in School and Clinic, 35*(1), 9–15.

Salend, S.J., & Taylor, L. (1993). Working with families: A cross-cultural perspective. *Remedial and Special Education, 14,* 25–32.

Sameroff, A., & Chandler, M.J. (1975). Reproductive risk and the continuum of caretaking casualty. In F.D. Horowitz, M. Hetherington, S. Scarr-Salapatels, & G. Siegel (Eds.), *Review of child development research* (Vol. 4, pp. 187–244). Chicago: University of Chicago Press.

Sameroff, A.J. (1993). Models of development and developmental risk. In C.H. Zeanah, Jr. (Ed.), *Handbook of infant mental health* (pp. 3–13). New York: The Guilford Press.

Sameroff, A.J. (1995). General systems theories and developmental psychopathology. In D. Cicchetti & D.J. Cohen (Eds.), *Developmental psychopathology: Theory and methods* (Vol. 1, pp. 659–695). New York: John Wiley & Sons.

Sattler, J.M. (1998). *Clinical and forensic interviewing of children and families.* San Diego: Author.

Scheve, P.A. (1998). Past, present, and future roles of child protective services. *The Future of Children, 8*(1), 23–38.

Schneider, H.J. (1993). Violence in the family. *Studies on Crime and Crime Prevention, 2,* 34–44.

Simon, P.A., & Baron, R.C. (1994). Age as a risk factor for burn injury requiring hospitalization during early childhood. *Archives of Pediatric Adolescent Medicine, 148,* 394–397.

Skuse, D., Reilly, S., & Wolke, D. (1994). Psychosocial adversity and growth during infancy. *European Journal of Child Nutrition, 480*(Suppl. 1), 113–130.

Slavin, R. (1991). *Educational psychology.* Upper Saddle River, NJ: Prentice Hall.

Slavin, R.E. (1995). *Cooperative learning: Theory, research, and practice.* Upper Saddle River, NJ: Prentice Hall.

Smith-Trawick, J. (2000). *Early childhood development: A multicultural perspective.* Upper Saddle River, NJ: Prentice Hall.

Snell, M.E., & Brown, F. (2000). *Instruction of students with severe disabilities.* Upper Saddle River, NJ: Prentice Hall.

Snell, M.E., & Janney, M. (2000). *Social relationships and peer support.* Baltimore: Paul H. Brookes Publishing Co.

Snyder, L.S., Nathanson, R., & Saywitz, K.J. (1993). Children in court: The role of discourse processing and production. *Topics in Language Disorders, 13*(4), 39–58.

Sobsey, D. (1994). *Violence and abuse in the lives of people with disabilities: The end of silent acceptance?* Baltimore: Paul H. Brookes Publishing Co.

Social Security Act of 1935, PL 74-271, 42 U.S.C. 301 §§ *et seq.*

Stermer, J. (1997, July 31). Home visits give kids a chance. *Chicago Tribune,* Section 1, 16.

Stipek, D. (1993). *Motivation to learn: From theory to practice.* Needham Heights, MA: Allyn & Bacon.

Strike, K.A., Haller, E.J., & Soltis, J.F. (1998). *The ethics of school administration.* New York: Teachers College Press.

Summerlin, K.L. (1990). Giving teen mothers a second chance at school. *Georgia Alert, 12,* 11–47.

Taylor, R. (2000). *Assessment of exceptional students.* Needham Heights, MA: Allyn & Bacon.

Terr, L. (1990). *Too scared to cry: Psychic trauma in childhood.* New York: Harper & Row.

Terr, L.C. (1991). Childhood traumas: An outline and overview. *American Journal of Psychiatry, 148,* 10–20.

Thorp, E.N., & McCollum, J.A. (1994). Defining the infancy specialization in early childhood special education. In L.J. Johnson, R.J. Gallaher, & M.J. LaMontagne (Eds.), *Supporting and strengthening families* (pp. 2–11). Cambridge, MA: Brookline Books.

Tower, C.C. (1992). *The role of educators in the protection and treatment of child abuse and neglect.* Department of Health and Human Services Publication No. ACF 92-30172. Washington, DC: U.S. Department of Health and Human Services, Administration for Children and Families, Administration on Children, Youth and Families, National Center on Child Abuse and Neglect.

Turnbull, A., Turnbull, R., Shank, M., & Leal, D. (1999). *Exceptional lives: Special education in today's schools.* Upper Saddle River, NJ: Prentice Hall.

Turnbull, H.R., Buchele-Ash, A., & Mitchell, L. (1994). *Abuse and neglect of children with disabilities: A policy analysis.* Lawrence: Beach Center on Families and Disabilities, The University of Kansas.

Tyree, C.L., Vance, M.B., & Boals, B.M. (1991). *Restructuring the public school curriculum to include parenting education classes.* Little Rock: Arkansas State University.

Tzeng, O.C.S., Jackson, J.W., & Karlson, H.C. (1991). *Theories of child abuse and neglect: Differential perspectives, summaries, and evaluations.* New York: Praeger.

U.S. Department of Health and Human Services. (1994). *Child maltreatment 1992: Reports from the states to the National Center on Child Abuse and Neglect.* Washington, DC: U.S. Government Printing Office.

U.S. Department of Health and Human Services, Children's Bureau. (1998). *Child maltreatment 1996: Reports from the states to the National Child Abuse and Neglect Data System.* Washington, DC: U.S. Government Printing Office.

U.S. Department of Health and Human Services, Administration for Children and Families, U.S. Advisory Board on Child Abuse and Neglect. (1991). *Creating caring communities: Blueprint for an effective federal policy on child abuse and neglect. Executive summary.* Washington, DC: U.S. Government Printing Office.

U.S. Department of Health, Education and Welfare, Head Start. (1977). Children's Bureau; Administration on Children, Youth and Families; Office of Human Development. *Child abuse and neglect: A self-instructional text for Head Start personnel* (Publication No. OHDS 8-31103). Washington, DC: U.S. Government Printing Office.

Unger, D.G., & Cooley, M.L. (1992). Partner and grandmother contact in black and white teen parent families. *Journal of Adolescent Health, 13,* 546–552.

United Nations. (1989). *United Nations convention on the rights of the child.* New York: Author.

Utley, C., Mortsweet, S., & Greenwood, C. (1997). Peer-mediated instruction and interventions. *Focus on Exceptional Children, 29*(5), 1–23.

van IJzendoorn, M.H., Juffer, F., & Duyvesteyn, M.G.C. (1995). Breaking the intergenerational cycle of insecure attachment: A review of the effects of attachment-based interventions on maternal sensitivity and infant security. *Journal of Child Psychology and Psychiatry, 36,* 225–248.

Vandercook, T., York, J., & Sullivan, B. (1993). True or false? Truly collaborative relationships can exist between university and school personnel. *OSERS News in Print, 5*(8), 3–4.

Vaughn, S., Bos, C.S., & Schumm, J.S. (2000). *Teaching exceptional, diverse, and at-risk students in the general education classroom.* Needham Heights, MA: Allyn & Bacon.

Vaughn, S., & LaGreca, A. (1993). Social skills training: Why, who, what, and how. In W.N. Bender (Ed.), *Learning Disabilities: Best practices for professionals* (pp. 251–271). North Potomac, MD: Andover Medical.

Voices for Illinois Children. (1999). *The charter for Illinois children.* Chicago: Author.

Vondra, J.I. (1990). Sociological and ecological factors. In R.T. Ammerman & M. Hersen (Eds.), *Children at risk: An evaluation of factors contributing to child abuse and neglect* (pp. 149–170). New York: Kluwer Academic/Plenum Publishers.

Vondra, J.I., Barnett, D., & Cicchetti, D. (1990). Self-concept, motivation, and competence among preschoolers from maltreating and comparison families. *Child Abuse and Neglect, 14,* 525–540.

Vondra, J.I., & Toth, S.L. (1987). Child maltreatment research and intervention. *Early Child Development and Care, 42,* 11–24.

Vygotsky, L.S. (1962). *Thought and language.* Cambridge, MA: MIT Press.

Vygotsky, L.S. (1978). *Mind in society: The development of higher psychological processes.* Cambridge, MA: Harvard University Press.

Walker, H.M., & Sprague, J.R. (1999). The path to school failure, delinquency, and failure. *Intervention in School and Clinic, 35*(2), 67–73.

Walker, J.E., & Shea, T.M. (1999). *Behavior management: A practical approach for educators.* Upper Saddle River, NJ: Prentice Hall.

Weinreb, M.L. (1997). Be a resiliency mentor: You may be a lifesaver for a high-risk child. *Young Children, 52*(2), 14–20.

Weissbourd, R. (1996). *The vulnerable child: What really hurts America's children and what we can do about it.* Reading, MA: Addison-Wesley.

Werner, E.E. (1990). Protective factors and individual resilience. In S. Meisels & J. Shonkoff (Eds.), *Handbook of early childhood development* (pp. 97–116). New York: Cambridge University Press.

Werner, E.E. (1995). Resilience in development. *Current Directions in Psychological Science, 4,* 81–85.

Westman, J.C. (1996). The child advocacy team in child abuse and neglect matters. *Child Psychiatry and Human Development, 26*(4), 221–225.

Williams, L. (1994). Developmentally appropriate practice and cultural values: A case in point. In B.L. Mallory & R.S. New (Eds.), *Diversity and developmentally appropriate practice* (pp. 155–182). New York: Teachers College Press.

Windsor, J. (1995). Language impairment and social competence. In S.F. Warren & Reichle (Series Eds.) & M.E. Fey, J. Windsor, & S.F. Warren (Vol. Eds.), *Language intervention: Preschool through the elementary years* (pp. 213–218). Baltimore: Paul H. Brookes Publishing Co.

Winton, P.J. (1996). Understanding family concerns, priorities, and resources. In P.J. McWilliam, P.J. Winton, & E.R. Crais (Eds.), *Practical strategies for family-centered intervention* (pp. 31–53). San Diego: Singular Publishing Group.

Yehle, A.K., & Rambold, C. (1998). An ADHD success story: Strategies for teachers and students. *Teaching Exceptional Children, 30*(6), 8–13.

Yoder, P.J., Kaiser, A.P., Goldstein, H., Alpert, C., Mousetis, L., Kaczmarek, L., & Fisher, R. (1995). An exploratory comparison of milieu teaching and responsive interaction in classroom applications. *Journal of Early Intervention, 19,* 218–242.

Youngblade, L.M., & Belsky, J. (1989). Child maltreatment, infant–parent attachment security, and dysfunctional peer relationships in toddlerhood. *Topics in Early Childhood Special Education, 9*(2), 1–15.

Young-Eisendrath, P. (1996). *The gifts of suffering: Finding insight, compassion, and renewal.* Reading, MA: Addison-Wesley.

Ysseldyke, J.E., & Thurlow, M.L. (1994). *Participation of students with disabilities in statewide assessment programs.* Minneapolis: National Center on Educational Outcomes, University of Minnesota.

Zeanah, C.H., & Scheeringa, M. (1996). Evaluation of posttraumatic symptomatology in infants and young children exposed to violence. In J.D. Osofsky & E. Fenichel (Eds.), *Islands of safety: Assessing and treating victims of violence* (pp. 9–14). Washington, DC: ZERO TO THREE Publications.

Zeanah, C.H., Jr. (1993). *Handbook of infant mental health.* New York: The Guilford Press.

A

RESOURCES FOR INFORMATION ABOUT CHILD MALTREATMENT

The following is a selection of resources that pertain to child maltreatment. This list is not designed to be evaluative, but, rather, it is designed to provide more information about the identification and prevention of child maltreatment. The resources consist of an annotated bibliography of books, journals, videotapes, and audiotapes.

BOOKS

Crosson Tower, C. (1999). *Understanding child abuse and neglect.* Needham Heights, MA: Allyn & Bacon.

This comprehensive book focuses on working with children who are abused and neglected. Some of the topics examined include family roles; the effect of maltreatment on child development; and the consequences of different types of abuse, including physical, sexual, and emotional abuse as well as neglect. In addition, interventions are described.

Donahue, P.J., Falk, B., & Gersony Provet, A. (2000). *Mental health consultation in early childhood.* Baltimore: Paul H. Brookes Publishing Co.

This book provides information about the changing role of early childhood education to include collaboration with mental health professionals. Center-based interventions with children who are at risk and parents who are difficult to reach are described, including crisis interventions for the impact that traumatic events might have on them, such as a death in the family or in the community, disaster, violence, and child maltreatment.

Johns, B.H., & Carr, V.G. (1995). *Techniques for managing verbally and physically aggressive students*. Denver, CO: Love.

This book describes practical techniques for the management of students who are verbally and/or physically aggressive. The techniques are especially geared to children with severe, challenging behaviors. Strategies for working with parents also are provided, and community agency involvement is highlighted.

Kemp, A. (1998). *Abuse in the family: An introduction*. Pacific Grove, CA: Brooks/Cole Thomson Learning.

This book, written for students and professionals, includes detailed descriptions of the historical basis for child abuse and neglect, types and causes of child maltreatment, the effects that abuse and neglect have on development, legal and ethical concerns, interventions, causes of domestic violence, and information on the maltreatment of older adults. All of the topics discussed are viewed with an ecological or systems perspective.

Koplow, L. (1996). *Unsmiling faces: How preschools can heal*. New York: Teachers College Press.

This book helps teachers realize that they can help young children who are maltreated to heal emotionally and socially. A curriculum based on fostering emotional development of children who are at risk is presented with lesson plans for teachers. Suggestions also are provided about how to assist the children's families. This book concludes with interventions for the helpers, such as teachers and other professionals, who may feel overwhelmed at times by the many challenges in their work.

Lambie, R. (2000). *Family systems within educational contexts: Understanding at-risk and special-needs students*. Denver, CO: Love.

This book provides detailed information on challenging family situations, community resources to assist families in need, and resiliency factors in children. It also emphasizes the necessity for school personnel to become healing influences on children who have suffered traumas from violence and maltreatment.

Monahon, C. (1997). *Children and trauma: A guide for parents and professionals*. San Francisco: Jossey-Bass.

This book teaches professionals the possible effects of trauma on children and the warning signs that indicate their need for assistance. A number of straight-forward interventions are suggested that can assist children in restoring their feelings of safety.

Reppucci, N.D., Britner, P.A., & Woolard, J.L. (1997). *Preventing child abuse and neglect through parent education*. Baltimore: Paul H. Brookes Publishing Co.

This book emphasizes the values of parent education and support systems in fostering competencies in parenting and coping skills. It also points out the necessity for additional research to learn more about the implementation of parent education programs, their long-term effectiveness, and the training of parent educators and home visitors. The authors encourage the adoption of a public policy to combat and eliminate child maltreatment.

Sattler, J.M. (1998). *Clinical and forensic interviewing of children and families: Guidelines for the mental health, education, pediatric, and child maltreatment field*. San Diego: Jerome M. Sattler.

This is a very comprehensive and detailed book that describes the following topics in depth: general principles for interviewing children with special needs, including those who have been maltreated, and their family members for clinical purposes and court procedures; methods of reporting and writing reports; and interventions that can be implemented by teachers and other professionals. This book is a valuable resource for service providers in the fields of education, mental health, pediatrics, law enforcement, and social work.

Smith, G.H., Coles, C.D., Kanne Poulsen, M., & Cole, C.K. (1995). *Children, families, and substance abuse: Challenges for changing educational and social outcomes*. Baltimore: Paul H. Brookes Publishing Co.

This book was written for teachers, other school personnel, and community service providers who assist children and families affected by substance abuse. Background information is first given about the characteristics of children whose families abuse drugs, and then interdisciplinary programs are proposed for effective interventions and services. Next, issues concerning addiction and treatments are described. Developmental needs of young children affected by family addiction are discussed, and a variety of classroom interventions are suggested. This book concludes with requirements for collaborative service systems and a presentation of a series of exemplary programs in the United States.

Walker, J.E., & Shea, T.M. (1999). *Behavior management: A practical approach for educators*. Upper Saddle River, NJ: Prentice Hall.

This book describes behavior management strategies for use by teachers in general, special, and inclusive classes. The strategies in this book are easy to understand and apply to students with challenging behaviors.

Zeitlin, S., & Williamson, G.G. (1994). *Coping in young children: Early intervention practices to enhance adaptive behavior and resilience*. Baltimore: Paul H. Brookes Publishing Co.

This book describes strategies that help children cope with problems by facilitating social interactions, problem solving, conflict management, and self-regulation of emotions.

JOURNALS

Child Abuse and Neglect
Elsevier Science Limited
Pergamon
Post Office Box 800
Kidlington, Oxford OX5 1DX
United Kingdom

Child Maltreatment
Sage Publications
2455 Teller Road
Thousand Oaks, CA 91320

Childhood Education
Association for Childhood Education International (ACEI)
17904 Georgia Avenue, Suite 215
Olney, MD 20832
E-mail: aceihq@aol.com

Disability and Society
Carfax Publishing Company
Post Office Box 25
Abingdon, Oxfordshire OX14 3UE
United Kingdom

Exceptional Children
Council for Exceptional Children
1920 Association Drive
Reston, VA 20191-1589
E-mail: cec.sped.org

Focus on Pre-K and K
Association for Childhood Education International
17904 Georgia Avenue, Suite 215
Olney, MD 20832
E-mail: aceihq@aol.com

The Future of Children
David and Lucy Packard Foundation
Center for the Future of Children
300 Second Street, Suite 102
Los Altos, CA 94022

Infants and Young Children
7201 McKinney Circle
Frederick, MD 21701

Infant-Toddler Intervention: The Transdisciplinary Journal
401 West A Street, Suite 325
San Diego, CA 92101-7904
E-mail: singpub@singpub.com

Intervention in School and Clinic
PRO-ED
8700 Shoal Creek Boulevard
Austin, TX 78757-6897
Web site: http://www.proedinc.com

Journal of Early Intervention
Division for Early Childhood
Council for Exceptional Children
1920 Association Drive
Reston, VA 20191-1589
E-mail: cec.sped.org

Journal of Emotional and Behavioral Disorders
PRO-ED
8700 Shoal Creek Boulevard
Austin, TX 78757-6897
Web site: http://www.proedinc.com

Journal of Learning Disabilities
PRO-ED
8700 Shoal Creek Boulevard
Austin, TX 78757-6897
Web site: http://www.proedinc.com

Journal of Positive Behavior Interventions
PRO-ED
8700 Shoal Creek Boulevard
Austin, TX 78757-6897
Web site: http://www.proedinc.com

Journal of Special Education
PRO-ED
8700 Shoal Creek Boulevard
Austin, TX 78757-6897
Web site: http://www.proedinc.com

LD Forum
Council for Learning Disabilities
Post Office Box 40303
Overland Park, KS 66204-4303

Learning Disabilities Quarterly
Council for Learning Disabilities
Post Office Box 40303
Overland Park, KS 66204-4303

Learning Disabilities: Research and Practice
Division for Learning Disabilities
Council for Exceptional Children
1920 Association Drive
Reston, VA 20191-1589
E-mail: cec.sped.org

Reclaiming Children and Youth
PRO-ED
8700 Shoal Creek Boulevard
Austin, TX 78757-6897
Web site: http://www.proedinc.com

Remedial and Special Education
PRO-ED
8700 Shoal Creek Boulevard
Austin, TX 78757-6897
Web site: http://www.proedinc.com

Teaching Exceptional Children
Council for Exceptional Children
1920 Association Drive
Reston, VA 20191-1589
E-mail: cec.sped.org

Topics in Early Childhood Special Education
PRO-ED
8700 Shoal Creek Boulevard
Austin, TX 78757-6897
Web site: http://www.proedinc.com

Young Children
National Association for the Education of Young Children
1509 16th Street NW
Washington, DC 20036-1426
E-mail: naeyc@naeyc.org

Young Exceptional Children
Division for Early Childhood
Council for Exceptional Children
1444 Wazee Street, Suite 230
Denver, CO 80202
E-mail: dec_execoff@together.cudenver.edu

VIDEOTAPES

*A Practical Book and Video Kit for Controlling the Angry Child
   at Home and at School*
Childswork and Child's Play
135 Dupont Street
Post Office Box 760
Plainview, NY 11803-0760

Avoiding Violence and Abuse
Childswork and Child's Play
135 Dupont Street
Post Office Box 760
Plainview, NY 11803-0760

Child Abuse: Cradle of Violence
MTI Film and Video
108 Wilmot Road
Deerfield, IL 60015

Child of Rage: A Story of Abuse
Ambrose Video Publishing
28 West 44th Street, Suite 2100
New York, NY 10036

Child Sexual Abuse: What Are You Going to Do About It?
Association for Childhood Education International
17904 Georgia Avenue, Suite 215
Olney, MD 20832

Children in Peril
Learning International
Post Office Box 10211
680 Washington Boulevard
Stamford, CT 06901-3709

Conduct Disorders of Children
Childswork and Child's Play
135 Dupont Street
Post Office Box 760
Plainview, NY 11803-0760

Healthy Children Today, Healthy Adults Tomorrow
Association for Childhood Education International
17904 Georgia Avenue, Suite 215
Olney, MD 20832

Incest: The Victim Nobody Believes
MTI Film and Video
108 Wilmot Road
Deerfield, IL 60015

Violence Prevention Package
Childswork and Child's Play
135 Dupont Street
Post Office Box 760
Plainview, NY 11803-0760

The following videotapes can be purchased from the publishers; however, they also are available for loan from The Illinois Early Childhood Clearinghouse, 830 South Spring Street, Springfield, IL 62704; E-mail: clearinghouse@eosinc.com:

A Look Into the Future. Sacramento, CA: Child Development Media, Inc.
A Teacher Saved My Life. Springfield: Illinois State Bar Association.
Child Abuse: Chain of Pain. Charleston, WV: Meridian Education Corporation.
Early Intervention's Response to Child Maltreatment: Indications, Reports and Follow Through. Macomb: Western Illinois University.
Factors in Parenting that Lead to Abusive Behavior. Charleston, WV: Meridian Education Corporation.
In a Different World: Understanding Social and Emotional Problems. Circle Pines, MN: American Guidance Service.
Johnson Family: Love Across the Generations: Grandmothers Caring for Grandchildren. Sacramento, CA: Child Development Media.
Preventing Sexual Abuse. New York: Young Adult Institute.
Psychoanalytic View of Abuse and Neglect in Infants and Children. Chicago: Illinois Association for Infant Mental Health.
Special Children: Special Risk. Boys Town, NE: Father Flanagan's Boys' Home.

AUDIOTAPES

Early Childhood Gang Intervention and Prevention Strategies
Association for Childhood Education International
17904 Georgia Avenue, Suite 215
Olney, MD 20832

*Empowering Children to Create a Caring Culture in a World of
Differences*
Association for Childhood Education International
17904 Georgia Avenue, Suite 215
Olney, MD 20832

Landmarks in Discovering the Human Dimension
Association for Childhood Education International
17904 Georgia Avenue, Suite 215
Olney, MD 20832

Treating the "Angry" Child
Childswork and Child's Play
135 Dupont Street
Post Office Box 760
Plainview, NY 11803-0760

*Working with Children Prenatally Exposed to Drugs: Implications
for Teachers*
Association for Childhood Education International
17904 Georgia Avenue, Suite 215
Olney, MD 20832

B

CONTACT INFORMATION
FOR ORGANIZATIONS

The following directory contains the names and addresses (postal, e-mail, and web site, if available) of a selection of organizations that work to combat child maltreatment. The list is not designed to be evaluative, but, rather, it is designed to assist individuals who need it with the contact information. This directory also includes some hotline telephone numbers for easy access.

American Humane Association
63 Inverness Drive East
Englewood, CO 80012-5117
E-mail: children@americanhumane.org
Web site: http://www.americanhumane.org

American Professional Society on the Abuse of Children (APSAC)
Post Office Box 26901
CHO 3B-3406
Oklahoma City, OK 73190
Web site: http://www.apsac.org

Association for Childhood Education International (ACEI)
17904 Georgia Avenue, Suite 215
Olney, MD 20832
E-mail: aceihq@aol.com
Web site: http://www.udel.edu/bateman/acei

Child Welfare League of America
440 First Street NW, Third floor
Washington, DC 20001-2085
Web site: http://www.cwla.org

Childhelp USA
15757 N. 78th Street
Scottsdale, AZ 85260
Web site: http://www.childhelpusa.org

The Children's Defense Fund
25 E Street, NW
Washington, DC 20001
E-mail: edinfo@childrensdefense.org
Web site: http://www.childrensdefense.org

The Council for Exceptional Children (CEC)
1110 North Globe Road, Suite 300
Arlington, VA 22201-3704
Web site: http://www.cec.sped.org

Covenant House Nineline (for kids in trouble)
800-999-9999

Domestic Violence Shelter Aid Hotline
800-333-SAFE

Early Childhood Intervention Clearinghouse
830 S. Spring Street
Springfield, IL 62704
E-mail: clearinghouse@eosinc.com

Educational Resources Information Center/Elementary and Early
   Childhood Education (ERIC/EECE)
805 W. Pennsylvania Avenue
Urbana, IL 61801-4897
Web site: http://www.ericeece.org

Family Support America (formerly Family Resource Coalition)
20 North Wacker Drive, Suite 1100
Chicago, IL 60606
Web site: http://www.familysupportamerica.org/content/
   home.htm

The Future of Children
300 Second Street, Suite 200
Los Altos, CA 94022
Web site: http://www.futureofchildren.org

Head Start
Administration for Children and Families
U.S. Department of Health and Human Services
Post Office Box 1182
Washington, DC 20013
Web site: http://www2.acf.dhhs.gov/programs/hsb

Incest Survivors Anonymous
Post Office Box 17245
Long Beach, CA 90807-7245

International Coalition on Abuse and Disability
Spectrum Institute
Post Office Box T
Culver City, CA 90230-0090

Kempe Children's Center
1825 Marion Street
Denver, CO 80218
E-mail: kempe@kempecenter.org
Web site: http://kempecenter.org

National Association for Children of Alcoholics
11426 Rockville Pike, Suite 100
Rockville, MD 20852
Web site: http://www.nacoa.net/index.htm

National Association for the Education of Young Children (NAEYC)
1509 16th Street, NW
Washington, DC 20036-1426
Web site: http://www.naeyc.org

National Center for Missing and Exploited Children
Charles B. Wang International Children's Building
699 Prince Street
Alexandria, Virginia 22314-3175
Web site: http://www.missingkids.com

The National Center for Victims of Crime (formerly National
  Victim Center)
2111 Wilson Boulevard, Suite 300
Arlington, VA 22201
Web site: http://www.nvc.org

National Center on Child Abuse and Neglect (NCCAN)
Administration on Children, Youth and Families
U.S. Department of Health and Human Services
Post Office Box 1182
Washington, DC 20013-1182

National Clearinghouse on Child Abuse and Neglect Information
330 C Street, SW
Washington, DC 20447
E-mail: nccanch@calib.com
Web site: http://www.calib.com/nccanch

National Coalition Against Domestic Violence
Post Office Box 18749
Denver, CO 80218
Web site: http://www.ncadv.org

National Committee to Prevent Child Abuse (NCPCA)
332 S. Michigan Avenue, Suite 1600
Chicago, IL 60604
Web site: http://www.childabuse.org

National Court Appointed Special Advocate Association (CASA)
100 W. Harrison Street
North Tower, Suite 500
Seattle, WA 98119
E-mail: inquiry@nationalcasa.org
Web site: http://www.nationalcasa.org

National Institute of Mental Health (NIMH)
6001 Executive Boulevard, Room 8184
MSC 9663
Bethesda, MD 20892-9663
E-mail: nimhinfo@nih.gov
Web site: http://www.nimh.nih.gov

National Organization for Victim Assistance (NOVA)
1730 Park Road, NW
Washington, DC 20010
E-mail: nova@try-nova.org
Web site: http://www.try-nova.org

Parents Anonymous
675 W. Foothill Boulevard, Suite 220
Claremont, CA 91711
E-mail: palmelendez@juno.com
Web site: http://www.parentsanonymous.org

Parents Anonymous Hotline
800-421-0353

Prevent Child Abuse Illinois
528 S. 5th Street, Suite 211
Springfield, IL 62701
E-mail: pcai@fgi.net
Web site: http://www.childabuse.org

Runaway Hotline
800-621-4000

Safe & Drug-Free Schools Program
Office of Elementary and Secondary Education (OESE)
400 Maryland Avenue, SW
Washington, DC 20202
E-mail: safeschl@ed.gov
Web site: http://www.ed.gov/offices/OESE/SDFS

Teen Challenge
3728 W. Chestnut Expressway
Springfield, MO 65802
E-mail: tcusa@teenchallengeusa.com
Web site: http://www.teenchallenge.com

Voices for Illinois Children
208 S. LaSalle Street, Suite 1490
Chicago, IL 60604-1103
E-mail: info@voices4kids.org
Web site: http://www.voices4kids.org

INDEX

Page numbers followed by *f* indicate figures; those followed by *t* indicate tables.

Abandonment, *see* Neglect
Absenteeism, *see* Truancy, as sign
 of neglect
Abuse, *see* Maltreatment
Abusers
 characteristics of, 22–23
 psychological consequences of
  disclosure, 56
 theories about, 18–21
Academic performance, 39–43
Accommodations
 behavioral supports, 107
 curriculum modifications, 107,
  127–128
 school environment, 126–127
Active listening, 87
Active Parenting Program, 99
Activity-based intervention,
 132–133
Adaptations, school environment,
 126–127
 see also Accommodations
Adlerian philosophy, 105
Adolescents
 dropping out of school, 42, 97
 effects of maltreatment, 6
 language delay, 37
 as mothers, 38, 96–99
 physical abuse, 42
 protective factors, 26
 self-esteem, 35
 signs of abuse, 15*f*
Adoption
 Adoption Assistance and Child
  Welfare Act of 1980
  (PL 96-272), 4*t*

Family Preservation and Support
 Services Act of 1993
 (PL 103-66), 4*t*
Advocacy
 for children's rights, 74–75
 competencies of advocates, 62–63
 defined, 59
 for early intervention, 65–66
 importance of, 59–60, 62
 for public policy changes, 71–73
 for research, 73–74
 for services, 66–68
 for teacher training, 70–71
Affect, deregulation of, 32
African Americans, family
 structure of, 89
African societies
 attitudes about disabilities, 91
 communication style, 93
Age, effect on parenting skills of,
 96–99
Aggression
 neglect, sign of, 14
 neurological development and,
  31
 peer aggression, 132
 physical abuse, sign of, 9, 104
 preschool children, 40
 psychological abuse, sign of, 12
 psychological effect of
  maltreatment, 32
 sexual abuse, sign of, 11, 40
 social effect of maltreatment, 34,
  104
Aid to Families with Dependent
 Children, 2